Found Anew

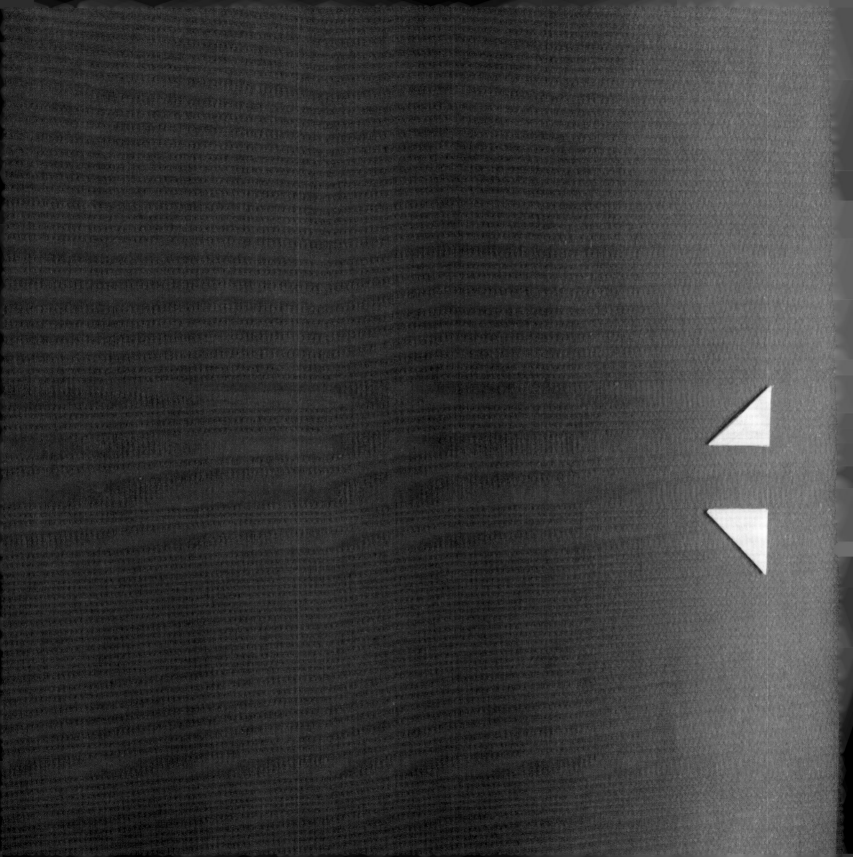

Found Anew

Poetry and Prose Inspired by
the South Caroliniana Library Digital Collections

EDITED BY

R. MAC JONES *and* RAY MCMANUS

THE UNIVERSITY OF SOUTH CAROLINA PRESS

Published by the University of South Carolina Press

Columbia, South Carolina 29208

www.sc.edu/uscpress

Manufactured in the United States of America

24 23 22 21 20 19 18 17 16 15
10 9 8 7 6 5 4 3 2 1

Library of Congress Cataloging-in-Publication Data
can be found at http://catalog.loc.gov/.

ISBN: 978-1-61117-564-6 (cloth)
ISBN: 978-1-61117-565-3 (paperback)
ISBN: 978-1-61117-566-0 (ebook)

Published in Cooperation with the South Caroliniana Library with the
Assistance of the Caroline McKissick Dial Publication Fund and the
University South Caroliniana Society.

STORY RIVER BOOKS

Pat Conroy, editor at large

PALMETTO POETRY SERIES

Nikky Finney, series editor

CONTENTS

List of Illustrations and Locations   vii

Talking with the Dead: A Foreword   xi
NIKKY FINNEY

Introduction   xiii

Renderings

The House and Surrounding Fields   3
ED MADDEN

Antebellum House Party   5
TERRANCE HAYES

Work   9
BRET LOTT

Washington Square, Charleston Tent City
after the Earthquake   11
MARJORY WENTWORTH

Interpreting Damage to a Huguenot Church
Documentary Photo   13
TERRI MCCORD

Fort Jackson Enlistees Meeting Sergeant   15
MARK POWELL

Stereoscopic View: The Circular Church   21
WORTHY EVANS

A Portrait of Two Women   23
THOMAS L. JOHNSON

Swamp Rabbit Parking Lot, Train in
Background   25
GILBERT ALLEN

Reimaginings

Railroad Alley   29
PHEBE DAVIDSON

The Art of Telling a Story about a Southern Family
Living in a Small Southern Town   31
WILL GARLAND

The Geologist Speaks of Phosphate   35
JOHN LANE

Pipeline   39
RAY MCMANUS

Train, Electric of Bob's   41
JILLIAN WEISE

The Cure   43
PAM DURBAN

Crib Death   51
CHARLENE SPEAREN

Freedman's School   53
MICHELE REESE

Humphrey   55
JULIA KOETS

Calling   57
GEORGE SINGLETON

Postcard from a Civil War Reenactment   63
RICHARD GARCIA

Possession   65
DANIEL NATHAN TERRY

The Curator   67
JANNA MCMAHAN

Impressions

Edisto Gothic   77
WILLIAM WRIGHT

Poem for Susan Lewis   81
SAMUEL AMADON

It's Time You Know Your People   83
JOHN MARK SIBLEY-JONES

A Brief History of Navigation   91
DARIEN CAVANAUGH

North   93
LAUREL BLOSSOM

11 Tanka for the Neighbors   95
JONATHAN MARICLE

August 1886   99
JULIA ELLIOTT

A Long Way Up   113
SUSAN LAUGHTER MEYERS

Aunt Gloriana's Amen Sunday   115
LINDA LEE HARPER

Contributors   117

LIST OF ILLUSTRATIONS AND LOCATIONS

All images are housed in collections at South
Caroliniana Library

*Photograph; The house and surrounding fields,
about 1908*   2
John Shaw Billings Papers, Photo Album 1, Accession
no. 7108
http://www.sc.edu/library/digital/collections/jsb.html

Dean Hall Plantation   4
Berkeley County Photograph Collection, Accession no.
1001.27, Folder 1001 Berkeley (23–43)
http://www.sc.edu/library/digital/collections/berkeleyweb.
html

Dean Hall Plantation   8
Berkeley County Photograph Collection, Accession no.
1001.44, Folder 1001 Berkeley (43–65)
http://www.sc.edu/library/digital/collections/
berkeleyweb.html

*[Washington Square, Charleston tent city after
earthquake]*   10
Charleston Earthquake 1886, Accession no. 11501.9
http://www.sc.edu/library/digital/collections/quake.html

*Charleston—Church—The Huguenot Church—Interior,
136–140 Church St.*   12
George LaGrange Cook Photograph Collection, Box 2;
Temporary num. 31
http://sc.edu/library/digital/collections/scook.html

Fort Jackson enlistees meeting sergeant   14
Curtiss B. Munn Photograph Collection, Accession no.
12941; Call No.: 12941.6
http://www.sc.edu/library/digital/collections/ww2.html

[Circular church after fire of 1861]   20
Stereographic Views of South Carolina, Call no. 6355.2
http://sc.edu/library/digital/collections/stereographs.html

Untitled Photograph   22
E. E. Burson Photograph Collection, Print no. 43, Folder 2
http://www.sc.edu/library/digital/collections/eeburson/

*Swamp Rabbit Parking lot, train in background,
Swamp Rabbit*   24
South Carolina Railroad Photograph Collection, Acces-
sion no. 14834.513
http://sc.edu/library/digital/collections/Railroads.html

Railroad Alley   28
Joseph E. Winter Collection, Accession no. 13025.2189,
Box 2
http://www.sc.edu/library/digital/collections/jwp

Callham Reunion, August, 1950   30
E. Don Herd Negative Collection, Reference no.
12499.222
http://sc.edu/library/digital/collections/herd.html

Phosphate rocks of South Carolina and the "great Caro-
lina marl bed," with five colored illustrations. A popular
and scientific view of their origin, geological position
and age; also their chemical character and agricultural
value; together with a history of their discovery and
development   34
Phosphates in South Carolina, 1870–1890, 553.64 P19
http://www.sc.edu/library/digital/collections/phosphate
.html

Train-car wreck   38
Beulah Glover Photograph Collection, Accession no.
12239.62, Folder 6
http://digital.tcl.sc.edu/cdm/singleitem/collection/bgp/
id/177/rec/94

Train. Electric of Bob's. August 1951   40
E. Don Herd Photograph Collection, Reference no.
12499.984
http://sc.edu/library/digital/collections/herd.html

Unidentified House—Iron banister   42
Marsh Photograph Collection, Folder 9883 15–33, Acces-
sion no. 9883–17
http://www.sc.edu/library/digital/collections/marsh.html

Ashley, Audrey—June 12, 1950, Belton, Infant in coffin
and grave   50
E. Don Herd Negative Collection, Reference no. 12499.45
http://sc.edu/library/digital/collections/herd.html

4 men with chickens   52
Harbison Agricultural College Collection, Accession no.
12525.43, Box 2
http://www.sc.edu/library/digital/collections/harbison
.html

Dog on horse   54
E. T. Start Photograph Collection, no. 57b, Sheet 3
http://www.sc.edu/library/digital/collections/start.html

Entrekin, Bill—(5) Negatives, Photographs of
family   56
E. Don Herd Negative Collection, Reference no.
12499.360
http://sc.edu/library/digital/collections/herd.html

House where Union officers were confined under fire,
Broad St.   62
Stereographic Views of South Carolina, Call Number
12612
http://sc.edu/library/digital/collections/stereographs.html

Charleston—Residence—Drayton Hall and 2 side
buildings   64
George LaGrange Cook Photograph Collection, Box 3;
Temporary num. 55
http://sc.edu/library/digital/collections/scook.html

Calm before the storm—white swans at
Brookgreen   66
Beulah Glover Photograph Collection, Accession no.
12239.78, Folder 9
http://sc.edu/library/digital/collections/glover.html

Beach Houses   76
   Beulah Glover Photograph Collection, Accession no.
     12239.30, Folder 3
   http://sc.edu/library/digital/collections/glover.html

Charleston—Church—Enston Home Chapel—Interior,
900 King St.   80
   George LaGrange Cook Photograph Collection, Box 2;
     Temporary num. 22
   http://sc.edu/library/digital/collections/scook.html

Untitled Photograph   82
   E. E. Burson Photograph Collection, Print no. 146,
     Folder 10
   http://www.sc.edu/library/digital/collections/eeburson/

Bateaus at dock, Edisto Park   90
   Beulah Glover Photograph Collection, Accession no.
     12239.31, Folder 3
   http://sc.edu/library/digital/collections/glover.html

Greenville County Rt. 25   92
   Marsh Photograph Collection, Folder 9883 180–198,
     Accession number 9883–183
   http://library.sc.edu/digital/collections/marsh.html

Family   94
   Armstrong Family Papers, 1900–1930
   http://digital.tcl.sc.edu/cdm/singleitem/collection/
     armstrong/id/176/rec/3

Miscellaneous—Residence—Interior—parlor   98
   George LaGrange Cook Photograph Collection, Box 5;
     Temporary num. 137
   http://sc.edu/library/digital/collections/scook.html

Page 5   112
   Harbison Agricultural College Collection, Accession no.
     12525.118, Box 1
   http://www.sc.edu/library/digital/collections/harbison.
     html

Street scene   114
   Beulah Glover Photograph Collection, Accession no.
     12239.38, Folder 4
   http://sc.edu/library/digital/collections/glover.html

I have long held close the habit of arguing with history but I have not often had the pleasure of talking with the dead, especially those who do not specifically, particularly, genetically, belong to me.

South Carolina history is far too often written down by those who believe they are worthy enough, wise enough, complete with aristocratic manners enough, to see everything that needs to be seen and remembered for, in their minds, all—who matter. This is of course not true. It takes many sets of eyes to get the whole truth.

Staring into the many different eyes of *Found Anew,* gazing into what is being held in the human hands in these many two-dimensional frames, I tilt my head in order to know just how the clothes of the time hung on the body of the time, moving from story to dusty street, back to poem, back to an old ironsides car, somewhat out of focus, that somehow exactly resembles another car of my life that once sat out in my grandfather's cow pasture, rusting away, when I was a girl. As I stare and turn the page without thinking I pause to talk with white men in work clothes who I would never stop and talk with in real life. I want to know from them, "What is it like to stand there and be there and not be able to jump one hundred years ahead to avoid conversation with me?" I want to ask the younger white girl in the corner

of a blurred frame, "What is your name and would you play with me?" I want to know, could I keep my own hair and complexion if we did?

In *Found Anew* I am deep in conversation with the dead. I'll admit it is a safe conversation, but it's a start. There's little risk anyone will misunderstand my curiosity and call me a name. There's little chance I will get something wrong and have to explain myself or hide. There's mostly wonder, space to re-imagine human beings filled with more truth than lies. There is also a beautiful silence, inside of which no one has to feel uncomfortable. I like the conversation this book makes me have. It is a conversation I don't get to have often enough in this day and time. This is always the power of art, creative spaces, and interpretation.

My modern staring and their unchanging reticent postures, their nineteenth-century bodies inviting or waving away my intrusive twenty-first-century eyes, ignite the rat-a-tat-tat of my insistent array of wonderings and questions. "Why doesn't she (who looks exactly like my Aunt Freddie) just put down the serving tray, walk fast out the back kitchen door, and not look back?" Or "who are those two black girls close inside each other's arms?" While turning the pages of this book I found myself *Star Trek*ed inside of my own poetic and highly imaginative diorama, moving in and around the four black men holding chickens in what looks like a school-yard. I was unwilling and unable to quickly turn the page. I thought to myself that my own students would fare far better in this world if they would put down their cell phones, pick up a chicken, and then figure out how to calmly hold it steady there while the camera snaps the moment for posterity. Perhaps my class lecture that day might begin with this: "Look at this photo, class, and tell me what you see?" In my *Star Trek* mind some smart arm would quickly shoot up into the air, followed by its anxious-to-be-right attached mouth and say, "I see fear," while another hand might shoot up and be followed by, "I see serenity. Calm." And then I would ask the class for their conclusion and surely some future visionary would answer, "We see what we want to see. We see what we need to see to not be afraid."

Found Anew has made me wonder if these personal and impulsive writings by a wide and impressive array of South Carolina-connected writers, inspired by images from a long time ago in South Carolina, might be the truest conversation that those of us from before can have with those of us from now. And perhaps, just perhaps, if we thought such a conversation was real and valuable and not some sidebar only for artists but rather a conversation we all could use, in order to imagine more about who and what we come from, perhaps we might one day finally move far, far away from all the old narratives that presently have us on REPEAT—narratives that have us do-ing what we want for the sake of only our own and

not doing what we need to do for the sake of a sacred geographical place that should be leaning far forward with a bounty of new narratives rather than leaning far back into the narratives of old. In other words, as so many great visionaries have already tried to tell us, we should follow the heart of the artist into the arena, trust-ing their lead, following their primary colors, their char-coal-stained fingers, as they point to where the evidence about who we are and what we come from, in order to map out new North and South poles.

It's true that sometimes our imaginations "run away with us," especially when we don't give ourselves over to the possibility of imagining something anew. But there are other times, if we are mindful, if we are open and alive to what we don't know but feel and see with more than our eyes, then our imaginations enter the room of a book filled with photographs, of people we don't know, of human moments frozen in time, of people who don't look like us, or who do, whose names we can't call, but who with a little help from the artists who live near and far, pen new voices on their lives. Perhaps when this happens we are able to do more than simply run away with our imaginations. Perhaps we are able to stretch our human wings out farther than we ever knew we could. Perhaps our physical human bodies and selves and not just our imaginations end up in absolute flight, high above the old narratives, high above and completely free of the official state sanctioned language of who we are and what on these shores was and is now possible. Then perhaps we too are found anew.

Nikky Finney

INTRODUCTION

In our South Carolina Studies classes, students research images to complement and complicate the South Carolina narratives they find in memoirs, histories, and historical newspaper articles, using collections of images made available online by the South Caroliniana Library. Students share their selected images in the classroom. Without knowing the specific who, what, where, when, and why of the creation of the image, students articulate initial impressions and questions based on personal reflections and cultural memories. Eventually, we come as close as we can, using information provided by the Library and our independent research, to the "real" context, to a more factual understanding of the history reflected in the image. But in our class conversations, we first let the images guide us. We wonder, *Does anyone else think that woman in the background looks sad?;* ask, *Is that what they would have worn all the time, or is it a special occasion?;* or inquire, *Would these folks have had ready access to a telephone at this time?* Sometimes our imaginations run away with us.

It was in the cab of a truck, talking over the new and exciting work that digital innovations have brought to our classrooms, that we couldn't help but wonder how our students' questions might be answered more creatively. What would happen if writers located an image, without knowledge of historical context, and simply wrote in response to it? We invited writers to this book project with more questions than goals. What would writers see in these collections? How would they approach the idea of "using" an image? How would they decide on an image to use? Would writers be inspired to create a response or would they feel compelled to invent what they felt was missing?

Inspiration takes forms and has demands that are often hard to pin clearly on either the source of the inspiration or the invention of the recipient. As we began to consider the shape of *Found Anew,* we knew that we wanted a simple prompt for contributors, one that would allow writers to fashion works that realized the potential in the South Caroliniana Library's digital collections in whatever form inspiration required. We sought out poets and fiction writers either born in South Carolina or whose strong ties to the state are evident in their creative output, and we asked them simply to browse the South Caroliniana Library's digital collections and select an image as inspiration for an original short story or poem.

The prompt did not include any formal statement on ekphrasis; the aim was not to try to capture the images in words in a prescribed manner. In truth, we aimed for eclecticism. We were more interested in the diversity of approaches to the collection that writers might take than we were in steering the writers toward a singular definition. We felt that this would allow a democracy to take place with the writer and image, and provide the freedom to explore and expand the idea of ekpharasis—how the writer arrived at the image and confronted it would be entirely up to the writer—and the hope was from the very beginning to allow writers a chance to take something old, perhaps forgotten, and make it new. We wanted to maintain that aim of the collection, beyond the obvious desire to showcase some exceptional work by gifted writers. While the digital collections are a well-used, and much valued, resource for researchers and educators, they might be more widely viewed as a source of inspiration for writers intent on inventing new narratives of South Carolina.

A simple prompt, certainly, but simplicity has its own way of producing challenges. By using this approach, writers produced works that are acts of discovery, rediscovery, and invention. Some writers gauged unlikely depths in images other eyes might pass over without second glances. Some radically recreated the context for the images, imaginatively removing the scenes from the times and spaces that they initially framed. Some gave us the perfect words for an impression, a feeling, or a hurt that resonates for us when we see certain pictures, but for which we could not ourselves find the right words. The images became for us not recovered or explained but *found anew.*

These writers produced work amazing, beautiful, and, at times, shocking. Reading the poem "Antebellum House Party" by Terrance Hayes or the short story "Work" by Bret Lott, one feels the power of the piece perfectly contained within the work itself, only to find the effect amplified by the facing image. Some writers find ways to flip initial perspectives we might have of an image—light becomes dark, and the past and the present blur—as in the pieces by John Lane, Ed Madden, William Wright, and Jillian Weise, where loneliness and isolation confound our understanding of space, both personal and public, and ask the reader to defy one without defying the other. The wide-eyed missionary in George Singleton's "Calling" coupled with the image becomes a comic tryst between the figurative and the literal. There were also the surprising echoes we had hoped to find in this collection. Julia Elliott's "August 1886" is a second-person tale that ruminates on the peculiarities of illness, which are only equaled by the oddness of what we find curative, and Pam Durban's "The Cure" is a story of the great lengths that one will traverse to find effective treatment and a reminder that what ultimately provides succor is often what we carry with us as we go.

The collections that the writers drew from are as varied as the works inspired by them. *Charleston Earthquake, 1886* demonstrates the devastation that would forever change the skyline of that port city. *Phosphates in South Carolina, 1870–1890* documents an often-overlooked boom of the late nineteenth century in South Carolina. *E. Don Herd Photograph Collection* is the product of a student at Belton High School in the 1940s and 1950s. *Beulah Glover Photograph Collection* and *E. E. Burson Photograph Collection* both collect the personal and professional pictures of studio photographers. *George LaGrange Cook Photograph Collection* comes from glass plate negatives. *Stereoscopic Views of South Carolina* gives us the double images meant to be layered in a stereoscope. *E. T. Start Collection* lenses Camden, S.C., while *Berkeley County Photograph Collection* captures another part of the State at the turn of the century. *Joseph E. Winter Collection* shows the streets of Columbia through thousands of photographs spanning six decades. *Harbison Agricultural College Photograph Collection* catalogues moments from a century of change from a college's founding until its closing. *South Carolina and World War II* and *South Carolina Railroads Photograph Collection* both draw from many sources to present a single subject with great breadth and depth. *Kenneth Frederick Marsh Photograph Collection* and *John Shaw Billings Photograph Albums, 1875–1939* are both eclectic collections that focus on a single location. With such a wide net and multiple avenues, writers could and did spend days, weeks, and months pouring over image after image. And even though the breadth of this collection allowed writers to wander in countless directions, their works share the effect of reminding us of the collective richness of individual histories that knit together to make South Carolina history.

A broad prompt allowed for such a varied collection, and yet, once collected, these works revealed commonalities in approaches to inspiration. The products of such an open call begged delineation into categories; we began to see that stories and poems in the collection could be thoughts of in three ways, as *Renderings, Reimaginings,* or *Impressions,* when considered alongside the images that acted as the sources of inspiration. While each short story and poem in the collection has attributes that might recommend it for any of these three appellations, and rightly so since the writers are looking through a

multitude of South Carolina images, it became apparent that these works, in the manner they were presented, fell into a distinct category organically rather than definitionally. Some works function primarily as close observations of the images, which is what one would expect with ekphrastic writing. But these works moved beyond recreating, and were more like *Renderings:* "The House and Surrounding Fields" by Ed Madden, "Antebellum House Party" by Terrance Hayes, "Work" by Bret Lott, "Washington Square, Charleston Tent City after The Earthquake" by Marjory Wentworth, "Interpreting Damage to a Huguenot Church Documentary Photo" by Terri McCord, "Fort Jackson Enlistees Meeting Sergeant" by Mark Powell, "Stereoscopic View: The Circular Church" by Worthy Evans, "A Portrait of Two Women" by Thomas L. Johnson, and "Swamp Rabbit Parking Lot, Train in Background" by Gilbert Allen.

Other works reimagine the context of the image and create a narrative beyond the frame. These works we saw as *Reimaginings:* "Railroad Alley" by Phebe Davidson, "The Art of Telling a Story about a Southern Family Living in a Small Southern Town" by Will Garland, "The Geologist Speaks of Phosphate" by John Lane, "Pipeline" by Ray McManus, "Train, Electric of Bob's" by Jillian Weise, "The Cure" by Pam Durban, "Crib Death" by Charlene Spearen, "Freedman's School" by Michele Reese, "Humphrey" by Julia Koets, "Calling" by George Singleton, "Postcard from a Civil War Reenactment" by Richard Garcia, "Possession" by Daniel Nathan Terry, and "The Curator" by Janna McMahan.

Along with works that rendered or reimagined, we were pleased to see works that captured a different sensibility in the image. They interpreted or imparted an impression of sentiment or promise. These we grouped as *Impressions:* "Edisto Gothic" by William Wright, "Poem for Susan Lewis" by Samuel Amadon, "It's Time You Know Your People" by John Mark Sibley-Jones, "A Brief History of Navigation" by Darien Cavanaugh, "North" by Laurel Blossom, "11 Tanka for the Neighbors" by Jonathan Maricle, "August 1886" by Julia Elliott, "A Long Way Up" by Susan Laughter Meyers, and "Aunt Gloriana's Amen Sunday" by Linda Lee Harper.

Several of the writers included in this anthology told us how hard it was to settle on a single image, and many intend to return to the digital collections as inspiration for writing beyond our anthology. This restlessness and promised return is heartening, certainly something we wanted out of the book project. A wellspring of fascinating and evocative historical images are easily accessible online, owing to the work of the *South Caroliniana Library* archivists, that can provide unique prompts for writing. We hope that *Found Anew* draws attention to this use for the digital collections as it provides a showcase for the original, innovative work of writers who have already found inspiration there.

R. Mac Jones
UNIVERSITY OF SOUTH CAROLINA–EXTENDED UNIVERSITY

Ray McManus
UNIVERSITY OF SOUTH CAROLINA–SUMTER

Renderings

ED MADDEN

House and surrounding fields, about 1908. John Shaw Billings Papers, Photo Album 1, Accession
no. 7108. Courtesy of South Caroliniana Library, University of South Carolina, Columbia, S.C.

The House and Surrounding Fields

Here, he stood here, at the foot
of the dirt road. The house lifted

above the fields like a boat. The fields
grew dark. The sky emptied itself

of whatever was once there.

The house glowed, pole star, the fields
and stubbled rows tilting round it. Was he

leaving? Was he returning? The house tilted
above the fields like an ark resting,

at last, here, in the brown fields,

the dove and crow long gone, nothing
but dust on the sills, the jamb, the drapes

drawn closed, no one watching, no one

waiting, to see. Was he leaving or returning?
Here, he stood here, the road a gash

on the face of the fields, and to his right,
at the fields' edge, three trees

like sentries, dark and vigilant.

Nothing grows between the seasons, between
then and now, nothing but dust and brown

light. The house drifts across the dark
fields, receding, like a beacon, like

a boat sinking in the distance, the road
like an itch, like a brown ribbon,

and him doing what he had to do.

Coffee after dinner, Dean Hall Plantation. Berkeley County Photograph Collection, Accession no. 1001.27, Folder 1001 Berkeley (23–43). Courtesy of South Caroliniana Library, University of South Carolina, Columbia, S.C.

Antebellum House Party

To make the servant in the corner unobjectionable
Furniture, we must first make her a bundle of tree parts
Axed and worked to confidence. Oak-jawed, birch-backed,

Cedar-skinned, a pillowy bosom for the boss infants,
A fine patterned cushion the boss can fall upon.
Furniture does not pine for a future wherein the boss

Plantation house will be ransacked by cavalries or Calvary.
A kitchen table can, in the throes of a yellow fever outbreak,
Become a cooling board holding the boss wife's body.

It can on ordinary days also be an ironing board holding
Boss garments in need of ironing. Tonight it is simply a place
For a white cup of coffee, a tin of white cream. Boss calls

For sugar and the furniture bears it sweetly. Let us fill the mouth
Of the boss with something stored in the pantry of a house
War, decency, nor bedeviled storms can wipe from the past.

Furniture's presence should be little more than a warm feeling
In the den. The dog staring into the fireplace imagines each log
Is a bone that would taste like a spiritual wafer on his tongue.

Let us imagine the servant ordered down on all fours
In the manner of an ottoman where upon the boss volume
Of John James Audubon's *Birds of America* can be placed.

Antebellum residents who possessed the most encyclopedic
Bookcases, luxurious armoires and beds with ornate cotton
Canopies often threw the most photogenic dinner parties.

Long after they have burned to ash, the hound dog sits there
Mourning the succulent bones he believes the logs used to be.
Imagination is often the boss of memory. Let us imagine

Music is radiating through the fields as if music is reward
For suffering. A few of the birds Audubon drew are now extinct.
The Carolina Parakeet, Passenger Pigeon, and Labrador Duck

No longer nuisance the boss property. With so much
Furniture about, there are far fewer woods. Is furniture's fate
As tragic as the fate of an axe, the part of a tree that helps

Bring down more upstanding trees? The best furniture
Can stand so quietly in a room that the room appears empty.
If it remains unbroken, it lives long enough to become antique.

BRET LOTT

Road to duck pond, Dean Hall Plantation. Berkeley County Photograph
Collection, Accession no. 1001.44, Folder 1001 Berkeley (43–65). Courtesy of
South Caroliniana Library, University of South Carolina, Columbia, S.C.

Work

The memory leaves. Walks away like a friend turned his back on you in your moment of need. But there are things won't go away. Better, and worse.

The worse I don't dwell much on now. No room in this crowded skull to comfort and aid the things have left my life. The children, Jackson, Theo and Caroline, all dead of their own old age. Of course Lissa, my joy, my bride, herself gone these thirteen years. But I will not dwell there. I loved them, still do. But I will not dwell there.

Instead, it is to the better things I repair: Seeing those children born and grown and married, then the grandchildren come after them. Grandchildren all grown now, past that the great grandchildren hither and yon, gone like chaff in a sharp wind. But I saw that, lived long enough—and longer—to know the name lives on, to see the smile on the babies' faces.

Another better thing: My bride when she lay back upon the bed our wedding night. Third floor of that Charleston hotel, a single candle, sea air soft through the open window. And the good thing, too, of her hand in mine when she passed in another bed, this in the home we lived in all our fifty-eight years.

Lissa.

And when of a night I lie awake for all the work it is to keep at bay the worse, me alone in this facility and serviced day in day out, just waiting my turn to plead my case before the Lord, I will see the better thing of woods in early morning. I will see the road ahead, my oldest boy, Jackson, beside me, we two headed toward the Cooper and the blind. I will feel shards of sunlight through the pine and cypress and live oak. I will smell the calm of the earth, the damp life of it, the wisps of morning fog in amongst the trees like ghosts afoot and lost. I will feel the weight of the gun crooked in my arms, startle at the surprise of a bird or deer or wild hog in the offing, then the shattering blast and acrid satisfied peace the smoke brings after.

The memory leaves: an old friend walking away. But some things stay: Lissa, the children. These woods I walk. Light, down through trees.

MARJORY WENTWORTH

Washington Square, Charleston tent city after earthquake, 1886. Accession 11501.9.
Courtesy of South Caroliniana Library, University of South Carolina, Columbia, S.C.

Washington Square, Charleston Tent City after the Earthquake

I no longer count the days
nor the long scorched nights passing
like lifetimes. As soon as sleep
finds me, I am running alone
through the dark, while walls crumble
and the earth rumbling low
like a wounded animal,
rises and pitches beneath me.

If not for the chimney bricks
falling fast from the sky
I would swear I was at sea,
like a small boat in a storm.
And this is how I feel
when I wake in the damp tent;
my husband snoring beside me,
the child inside my belly
flipping like a confused fish.

I light a candle and walk
outside. The moon hanging low
brightens the September sky,
and I almost believe what they say
about the world not ending.
I count the stars as if they are
my blessings, tip-toe back inside,
and touch the things we salvaged
stacked on a table: my brush
and comb, one silver candlestick,
the family Bible missing
its heavy brown cover.

TERRI MCCORD

Huguenot Church interior, 136–140 Church St. By George LaGrange Cook. George LaGrange Cook
Photograph Collection, Box 2; Temporary num. 31. Courtesy of South Caroliniana Library,
University of South Carolina, Columbia, S.C.

Interpreting Damage to a Huguenot Church Documentary Photo

See the seemingly   seared contact sheet
you a seer, please,   a bystander, by and by

the photographer's   intent from 1880,
no?   a grand   designer's plan,
for this age reveals   created work my eyes
lit upon. Make of this church what you will.

Imagine emulsion   that is perfect
for right now.   Press your fingers
on closed eyelids.   Lightly on the cornea.
The mind's eye   creates fractals. Or orbs
in an outer space.   This scanned image
how far removed?   of the damaged print
is a miracle,   a magic mirror, to reflect—

reflect— reflect on,   see beyond broken glass,
batiked plane, I repeat myself, yes?—   Eschered
    shapes, ah
what is safe—   to the snake's head to the left,
winged negative areas,   scattered black grackles, or
flushed-out coveys.   Enlarge and trace the crackling,
calligraphy between   dried mud tracks, crazed lines
in the abstract. Focus   down to a hornet's nest,
    aroused bees
or a dervish, but, no fear,   they are contained   here.
See beneath time   to the concrete—
the pews, the wood,   books, and the chandelier.
Still, I can't resist   the altar organ pipes
as a monarch's crown   and what has become
collaborative—   a mosaicked overlay of spiraled souls.

Fort Jackson enlistees meeting sergeant. By Curtiss B. Munn. Curtiss B. Munn Photograph Collection, Accession no. 12941; Call No.: 12941.6. Courtesy of South Caroliniana Library, University of South Carolina, Columbia, S.C.

Fort Jackson Enlistees
Meeting Sergeant

He kept it with him because it was civilized when all else was not. There were other things, of course, but on these he could not look. In England, yes. Even wading into France, days behind V Corps, days late, but close enough still to hear the 88s in shrill decline. But the others—photographs of faces, photographs of people he felt certain he had once known (and *loved?* had he loved them? Yes, had and would again; there's a woman in there, a photograph of her, hair in plaits)—the others remained buried in his pack, ruined, he suspected, by snowmelt. If the goddamn snow would ever melt.

He'd been in Bayeux, barely off the lip of the beach, for months, all of that lovely summer and fall of 1944 when, just before Christmas, word came of the breakthrough miles to the south in Bastogne. But he was Signal Corps. Two years of college back at Central Wesleyan. As if he'd ever intended to spend his life bent in the corn patch or following the traces of a mule, his daddy at the turn-row, coughing and spitting chew. No, sir. No, thank you. He was an educated man. He could even type. Taking a jeep to town—everybody loved him in town—and then he sees an MP he knows or knew

and buddy he is flagging him down, arms waving. Let me in, turn around, get back. We're moving.

Who is?

All of us.

To where?

Just go, come on.

He doesn't slow, doesn't speak until they are back on base and then he turns to the MP but buddy, he is already jumping out, that MP whose name he will never forget but can't remember either, he is already running.

Get your shit together, he is yelling, yelling and running and just not stopping and in his mind he is running still. In his mind he never stopped. Get your shit together, he is saying. We're headed to the line.

And that night they did. The chaplain blessing them as they filed onto a waiting C-47. The man throwing holy water and right then you knew it was bad, the way he flicked it from his fingertips. The sting of it in the winter air. They filed forward. Shuffle-step, stop. Shuffle-step, stop. Someone mooed like a cow but there was no heart in it. Everybody knew. I sat down on the carpet, six, seven years old, and pushed a fire truck from my knees and felt the warmth of the fire and the garland and the hung stockings and I thought about that, about how everyone knew.

If you look at it now, as I sometimes do, if you take it from his hand, stiff as it is—hand, photograph, everything has crimped—you will find him on your extreme right and what you might notice is how soft he appears, his face, the paunchiness only hinted at by the gathers in his suit. Oh, Lord, how it was then. You remember, Marion? You remember how it was then? Marion remembers. With him are his fraternity brothers. Sigma Nu. All from his pledge class. The five of them barely ensconced in college before they are leaving it, waving goodbye, a brass band on the quad playing Sousa, the girls waving. Gone for soldiers. Two dead in France before you ever even thought to wonder about them. Christ, how quick. They came from money, good families in Greenville, cars, books. Two years on the Sigma porch with your Latin and a tumbler of Elijah Craig. They had names if anyone cares to remember.

It wasn't like that for him. He didn't come from money. Not that he came from the absence of money. His daddy had eighty acres of bottomland and who knew how much pasture for grazing, enough to break your heart come time for baling, which came and came again. It was a closed world, that much he knew, that much he remembered still. They made the trek to Riverside once a week, hauled everything they had to the sales. It was a closed world but what he had against it he no longer recalled. The way the sweat gathered to bead his upper lip? There was that, yes, and he remembers too going

barefoot in the creek where the fat horny head waited in the deeper pools, angry barbed things. You cut the engine of the tractor and went to sleep with the sound of that old Farmall rattling around, caught in the ear like creek water gone warm. And then her. There is that woman whose photograph he carries and she will coalesce years later as my mother but for now she feels useless, a sentimental impulse you got to shed, brother. Like water left in a vase long after the flowers have died.

Dewey, if you remember Dewey and the way he always cocked that hat, Dewey was in intelligence. VII Corps somewhere south of here when a shell airburst and it was the trees that got him. A scattering of frozen limbs and trunks. He didn't know about the airbursts at first. They got off that C-47 in the middle of the night, short flight, so much shorter than he had wished it, and started walking up a road that would've been frozen had the tracks and wheels of an entire army not churned it. Two, three in the morning, and as they pass one man is handing out cartons of cigarettes and another a cartridge belt full of rifle rounds and you've got one in one hand, one in the other, fingers too cold to fiddle open your field-pack. You never stop moving. Up ahead a man is slopping food, beef—you feel the heat of it still, years later in the glow of Marion's study—onto a tin tray and you don't stop then either and maybe now would be the time for some cut-up son of a bitch to make that mooing sound but no, nobody is doing that. You just keep going forward, strung out in a line of typists and cooks and mechanics and anybody pretty damn much with two feet and a functional trigger finger. Going into the line as infantry replacements. Tomorrow somebody says something about Dewey and all you say is goddamn. Don't judge him. He didn't know what else to say any more than you.

Carson wore spectacles as he liked to call them. His daddy a chemist with a shop near the old Palmetto cotton warehouse. They lose track of each other after advanced training at A. P. Hill, different battalions, different lives. Carson sent to England while he was sent first to San Francisco for coastal defense and then on to England himself to the East Midlands but by then where was Carson and honestly did anybody care? When you see him twenty-odd years later at a reunion you find out he never went further east than London and that's fine, you don't judge a man for that, except to judge him lucky, but still you go and find Marion and point across the ballroom of the Holiday Inn and say You believe that son of a bitch had the nerve to come over and ask me what it was like. And Marion tips his drink and he can't believe it either, Marion can't.

Marion, who stands in Carson's shadow, is beside you.

Or in front of him, actually as they trudge forward. They think they are tired but they don't know tired, not yet. They think they are cold, but—we all know how this ends don't we? That's the thought running through his mind. Rushed forward, barely armed, barely trained. Fingers meant for the encryption keys of a radio. They have light weather capes and field jackets meant for spring. He tries to catch sight of Marion, three, four people in front of him and now and then he can. It's dark but here and there along the plowed road are burn barrels or two-and-a-half-ton trucks rushing past. Make-shift tents. Electric torches. Aid stations pushed off into the trees. Lit like ships at night but you can't see into them because God knows he tries. But instead up there is Marion, steady Marion (it is Marion I will drive my father to see, December after December, because only then does my father *not refuse,* to speak, to look, Christ, to listen!). Lost track of him after Virginia but then by great good fortune met up again in Suffolk and have been together ever since. Remember that night with them girls from Piedmont College? Remember that party, where was that, Marion, out near the river in Clemson, it must have been. His daddy stood with him the evening before he left for basic—was Marion there then, why the thought of Marion?—but his daddy, there in the gloaming. It was the first time he ever realized his daddy was old, or at least getting older, that this terror of earth and salt would someday die.

I know I ain't always done right by you, his daddy saying this.

But he doesn't want to hear this.

I know there's been things, son.

He doesn't want to hear this.

Night is coming. Soft Carolina spring. Fried catfish. His mamma's hush puppies like cake. Honeysuckle and the 3-in-One oil on his daddy's fingers. Up ahead machine oil is burning. He smells it, a big truck burning all the way down to the tires and nobody doing a thing about it. The whole world here and not a one of them doing a thing about it. They walk past. He's got the food in his mouth now, the cigarette carton in one pocket. The rounds in the cartridge belt he doesn't know what to do with. It is the most simple of things—sling it over your shoulder, young son!—but he can't manage even that. Hasn't fired a rifle in how long? But all the useless shit you memorized down at Jackson. The M1 Garand. 5.2 pounds unloaded. 5.8 loaded with sling. All that useless shit bubbling up until you see a man is dead under a green tarpaulin. Or something is beneath a green tarpaulin. Staked down but no, it's frozen in place, curved across the topography of face and chest, and legs and a single straying hand creeped out like a dead spider. You walk right on by it. Every one of you do. You head east.

We head north. Every December 21st from the time I am six—oh, the thrill those first years, mamma's silent disapproval and the smell of daddy in the car: Colgate shaving cream and KIWI heel & sole—until I am fifty-six I ride and then drive you north late at night through the peach fields stippled with frost, and then paved over for Direct Factory Outlets, north across the state line to Hillsborough, a hamlet with a pickle factory and a post office until—like the peach fields—that too has disappeared, this time beneath the aggregated weight of retirees from the Research Triangle with their degrees from Duke and TIAA-Cref accounts. They bury the town in antique shops and meat-and-threes that keep showing up in the pages of *Southern Living* but Marion doesn't move and we keep going, and I never mind.

They take trucks forward into the night, east, pile out just before dawn. The ground is too cold to dig but they dig it out anyway. Deep as you can get, boys. After sunrise someone comes by with hot chow and someone else comes by and says Did you hear about Dewey? You remember Dewey, don't you?

That boy in the middle, name of Hollis, had that cute girl liked him, Shelley, parents old Church of God folk so that she always had to slip out. Well, it was Hollis sent into the Hurtgen Forest and fuck you for asking, Carson.

But nobody knew that then. There was wonder enough that the sun rose. And nothing else happened. All day nothing else happened. Up and down the line, north to south, they could hear fighting but they are left untouched and really isn't that the worst of it? They sat in their foxholes and watched the treeline, the open field across which Panzers never came. Sometime in the afternoon soldiers started filling in the gaps, infantry replacements like themselves, because isn't this where the push will come? right here where nothing has touched? My mother told me a story later about my father watching the treeline. 1961. I was a boy, and my daddy, out looking for a little white face calf separated from its mamma, locks up, his eyes fixed on the far line of barbed wire out on the back forty and when mamma goes out there come dusk he pulls her down beside him and together they just lie there and watch and wait and nothing happens and finally nothing happens and he just gets up and together they walk back to the house and say never speak of it until, years later, mamma whispers it to me outside the church.

I can find no record of the sergeant to whom they reported. Or I can find record of ten thousand sergeants. Which is basically saying the same thing.

Artillery in the night. The Remnants of the 342nd Signal Corps, the lucky ones—remember?—pressed down into their holes. 88s. Mother of God. They burst in the trees and burst in the snow and the thing is to press yourself flat into the earth, *below* the earth, but even that doesn't matter if it's an airburst. The sudden *thwick* of a shattered tree. You get splinters big as your forearm. Men so prickled in death they appear olive porcupines, quills raised, hackles. If it wasn't frozen it would have smelled like the time daddy got cross ways and killed them dogs with his shovel. And Dewey. Goddamn, Dewey. They say you broke like ice. But in the morning he claws up out of his hole and who is left along his ravaged section of line but Marion. Good old Marion, standing up to stretch his cramped back, his fingers, just like your own, still wrapped around his cartridge belt, all those bullets he has yet to fire.

My wife walks into the kitchen, our daughter finally asleep.

It's too late to drive up there, she says. Go in the morning.

We always go up late. Get there at morning.

It's ridiculous.

It's how we've always done it.

Jesus, she says, he barely says a word to you or anyone and you run around like you're his chauffeur.

I watch her walk upstairs and then I drive over to pick up my father.

It's near dawn when we arrive and when he takes out the photograph I try to catch a glimpse of it but don't. When he dies years later I think to give it Marion but decide instead to keep it. Meanwhile, Marion sits in his wheelchair unattended and weeps.

The Panzers come through the sticks just after breakfast. You retreat, you run, everybody is running except some appear to be just lying there, not running. Not—and your eyes get that glaucous look and possibly it is the winter sun behind us through the kitchen windows and possibility it is not, but you don't finish the sentence and I don't ask you again.

After college I go to Eger because that is where you find yourself on V-E Day. I carry wine in my backpack, six liters of it, and it all turns in the July heat. It turns sour. I bring back Polaroids you refuse to look at. You have a wife and children and then grandchildren and they are in college and then out and still you move silently around the edges of that silence, refusing everything, refusing, when I ask, to name even the cold.

Circular Church after fire of 1861, Charleston. By George N. Barnard. Stereographic Views of South Carolina, Call no. 6355.2. Courtesy of South Caroliniana Library, University of South Carolina, Columbia, S.C.

Stereoscopic View

THE CIRCULAR CHURCH

A church that is circular is congregational.
Anyone who knows what a circle is
can be a minister.
A minister's particular parsing can involve rivers
that motion themselves into fires. A minister
can declare any person of any variety
a Congregationalist, one with us in a union. The notion
that a person can fit into any circle
is no more new than it was in 1861.
Sash factories in 1861 are flammable. This is a fact,
but there can be more. I can consider
that a Congregationalist can make enemies
of a sash factory owner , grounded in any sin
that can be considered deadly:
pride, envy, gluttony, lust, anger, greed, sloth.
I can consider that with these embers
a Congregationalist can start a fire.
Just one year before, in a square meeting place
down the street from the Circular Church,
candidates wrapped in sashes set fire to the nation

with circular logic on pretty paper. They spun around
and shot bullets in the air, then sent their oblation
to every newspaper around
that would print such stuff that plunged
a state into oblivion. The sash factory fire
is a simple asterisk to this.
The city between rivers felt its stucco
become brittle. The smell of wood and rot
burning from the firestorm permeated
a holy city. The dome of the church
plunged into its congregation and left
a ghostlike brick-and-mortar ring.
The city was ringed with shadows when the state
returned to a union. Bloated
with unexploded firebomb shells, the city
came back to a union too.
Over time, a dome capped the church again
for a minister to rise from a congregation
and call.

THOMAS L. JOHNSON

Unknown family, by E. E. Burson. E.E. Burson Photograph Collection, Print no. 43, Folder 2.
Courtesy of South Caroliniana Library, University of South Carolina, Columbia, S.C.

A Portrait
of Two Women

Though buried a long time ago, no doubt, six feet
under, left for dead, wept over in some country
churchyard, or in the cemetery on the edge of town,
their graves marked with simple but dignified stones,
they are buried no longer. Alive in their eyes on
    this paper,
this photograph. Alive in their smiles, the way they sit
together facing the camera, the music, the man
    snapping
the picture. Alive in their dress, one with lace on her
    sleeves,
locket around her neck (whose image might be there?),
the other in her best brown velvet dress showing off her
prized jewelry, gold or silver against the rich dark folds
of her breast. Found again. Discovered in the way
    they hold

themselves, the way they hold each other in intimacy
comfortably shown. The one on the right
leans in towards the other. They have found me,
taken me in, made me fall in love with them.
All the while I've been creating this new portrait
of these two, the young woman on the left has held
a fold-out camera in her lap, as if to say, "I too
would like to capture you, to take your picture,
give you a name, a place, maybe even give you back
your life, make something of you. Have you, like us,
stake a claim upon the future." I wonder if they
    might like
a chance to have me pose against a wall and shoot me
there. A vine-covered wall with a big black hole in it
where the emulsion on the photographic plate
has peeled off, leaving a part of the picture lost forever.

GILBERT ALLEN

Swamp Rabbit Parking lot, train in background, Ben Roberts Railroad Collection.
South Carolina Railroad Photograph Collection, Accession Number 14834.513. Courtesy of
South Caroliniana Library, University of South Carolina, Columbia, S.C.

Swamp Rabbit Parking Lot, Train in Background

The cop car tells me we're in Echo Valley,
1964 or thereabouts:
TERRITORIAL MARSHAL mimicking
the Golden Age of Television cowboys

and theme parks like the one outside the frame.
The hitching rails, the sanitized saloons,
mock gunfights, hangings interrupted by
a shot that shears the rope. But inside? There's

a man half cut off by the western edge
and a short woman, half cut off by him.
She holds a wicker handbag big enough
to get her started in another life.

The train's first car looks full; the second, empty.
Beyond the treeline, storm clouds fill the sky.
But in the foreground's world of gasoline
there's still enough sunlight to cast deep shadows.

Someone, perhaps the marshal, rests his palm
upon his trusty hood, as if remembering
a horse. And at the eastern edge, behind
the Rambler wagon, a toddler in short pants

stands with his own incongruous dignity.
To onlookers, the mom holding his hand
could be Camelot's Jackie on a bad
hair day. She gazes toward the ancient train

filling the past and future with its smoke.

Reimaginings

Railroad Alley, Columbia, S.C. Joseph E. Winter Collection, Accession no. 13025.2189, Box 2.
Courtesy of South Caroliniana Library, University of South Carolina, Columbia, S.C.

Railroad Alley

Walking cross-track after work.
Truth is, don't no one see the houses. Every
one just like the other, some of 'em
leaning hard, some a little bit straighter than
you'd think. Place where I grew up.
August like Hades in a handbag. Winters cold
as a witch's tit. One night some boy
come in our house and thought he was home.
We kept him 'til sunup next day. His
mama walked out hollerin' his name to tell
us whose he was. Late forties. Coulda
been anywhere USA. Us just kids and tracks
running straight to somewhere else,
at least please God not here. Whenever we
got a penny we put it on a rail, making
something slick and smooth. Them rails run
parallel here to there, the two tracks side
by side. We followed them once, to another
town, so much the same as to make no
mind. One like the other, the other like mine.
My brother stayed but I turned back.
Now hunker down by me. Listen close. Hear
those rails? The way they hum? Ain't
nothin' even coming, and the damned old rails
still hum.

WILL GARLAND

Callham Reunion, August, 1950. E. Don Herd Negative Collection,
Reference no. 12499.222. Courtesy of South Caroliniana Library,
University of South Carolina, Columbia, S.C.

The Art of Telling a Story about a Southern Family Living in a Small Southern Town

If you decide to sit down and tell a story about a southern family from a small southern town, you have to understand a few things. Start with the important stuff. Tell that part of the story right off, and tell it well. Try and make it yours. You are telling folks about your family, and there are enough crazies in your family to keep you from having to steal from other folks. But you should also just know that it won't ever truly be yours. Southern people have been telling their stories long before they even became southern people. And a lot of them thought to write them down.

When your aunt sat down to tell you about your family, she couldn't help but throw your family's stories in with the scripts of *The Help* and *The Divine Secrets of the Ya-Ya's*. It's not her fault. Don't be cross with her. Just leave those parts out and move on. She couldn't help it. She just identified too much with glitz and glamour of the Hollywood starlets, when they come down here and sweat till they glistened. Your aunt wanted to move to Hollywood one time, which probably explains a lot.

So like I said, don't get cross with her, just listen to her—try and catch her cadence, that's how you're going to capture her story anyway. And once you leave her house, go back to talk to your momma, and let her wade you through all of the nonsense until you figure out what ought to be kept.

But even then, realize that you are just going to be telling a story that is just a few degrees off from some other southerner that is trying to find the best way to tell their story. Flannery O'Connor grew up down the road from you. Your momma used to climb the pecan trees on her farm while her daddy talked to Flannery about her legal affairs. She knew how to tell a story. And you knew that you should read all of her stories if you ever hoped to figure out how to tell one of your own. That's how this whole mess started for you. You read her stories, and thought you should tell yours. But you never thought about how your words would be forever linked to hers. You just thought about those pecan trees and the times that your momma talked about how mean those peacocks were, and how they would chase her. But you learned about her from your family's stories, and you relished in her words until your words could pretend to sound like hers.

Forget her words.

Throw them off your desk with the rest of the drafts. They will still be there anyway. In a jumbled mess on the floor, waiting for you to stumble over them on your way to refill your coffee mug that says, "Write Like a Mother-fucker," because you know that you still need catchy little mantras if you want to have any hope of making this writing thing work as a career. Remind yourself that you have a wife and kid. You are doing this for them. This reminder will motivate your lazy ass to write. And when that doesn't work, look down at your over-priced mug and keep typing.

Some of Flannery's words will still find their way into your work. And your aunt will still sound a bit like Ashley Judd. But don't let this worry you too much. The crazies might be your own, but the stories are all a bit inbred. They feed on one another, no matter how much you try to separate them. After all, it is the same land that grew each of these stories. Your story doesn't make any sense without their story. It is just all a matter of finding your own way into this ongoing production that is so large that you never even sit back to think of it in those terms. It's like setting your family photo from Christmas up next to some other family's Christmas photo. They both have that cheap wood paneling that was all the rage back then. Both of them caught the youngest hiding back behind an uncle. Both of them are under exposed. But they're still different. Even with the youngest hiding

her face, and the rest of the faces darkened by the shadows, they are still different photos, with different histories that lead them into that moment. That's the way you go about telling your story.

And the other thing that you need to remember is that southern stories and stories about southern families living in small southern towns, by their very nature, are never linear. They are like those family photos. Each time you sit back down to look at them again, your eye drifts over some of the same, but it always ends up catching something new. There is a science to it, and while you don't need to worry too much about that, you do need to realize that there is a value in digressions and going back over the same material a few times. If a story is worth telling, the hearing of it is worth a little work.

So when it's all said and done, and you sit down to tell your story—don't hold back on the important stuff. Go ahead and let that spill out. After you do that, you can let the story tell itself. Let it take on a life of its own. It will want to do it anyway. You just sit back and let it happen. But you should realize that your story doesn't mean anything unless you can figure out some tiny glimmer of truth from the other stories all around you. Once you do that, then you can go back to your story. See what it's been doing. You let it roll of your tongue again, and see how it sounds—see what it looks like. Just like that photo, if you look at it enough times you will finally see that thing that someone else saw the first time.

That's how you tell your story. You sit down and you tell it. You let it tell itself. You don't covet their stories. There is plenty of room in the photo for all of the story-tellers. You just have to remember that.

Phosphate rocks of South Carolina and the "great Carolina marl bed," with five colored illustrations. A popular and scientific view of their origin, geological position and age; also their chemical character and agricultural value; together with a history of their discovery and development. Phosphates in South Carolina, 1870–1890, 553.64 P19. Courtesy of South Caroliniana Library, University of South Carolina, Columbia, S.C.

The Geologist Speaks
of Phosphate

They were lucky to mine what once was only ooze,
a mineral that looks like (is) fish roe, a gold strike
for the men who found it, who owned it, by hook
    or crook

or quick claim deed, now history, photos on a web site,
a footnote in a geology book. But without that ooze
we would not exist. By us I mean me, you,

New Carolinians, the whole of the now old New South.
In that ooze began one of many new beginnings—
not an oil strike like Texas, but phosphate, rich,

but a short lived commodity— ancient fish shit
in veins 6 to 36 inches thick, settled in shallows
by Oligocene, Miocene, and Pliocene tides and
    currents,

a geologic jackpot spread like mayonnaise below,
the buried economic beginning after the end,
at least for farming, as post-war entrepreneurial

clod-hoppers donned their slouch hats, abandoned
40-acres and a mule, dropped their hoes, strode out
of cotton fields and found in rich mineral seams

an extravagance of profit, a future—from farmer
to middle-man to Boss Man investor in cotton mills
and railroads, shiny-suited merchants selling wagon-
    loads

of fertilizer to neighbors for cotton acres of gullied
upcountry, slick-talking know-it-alls on mule-back
in mid-state sandy ridge fields selling porch-to-

porch their miracle of agricultural productivity,
maybe not a revolution in human purpose, but for
sure in wealth, geology intersecting with sociology

right here, one strike in a straight line
of South Carolina boom and bust economies
playing out geologist James Hutton's "we find no

vestige of a beginning,—no prospect of an end,"
not to the earth's record in rock but to somebody's
get rich quick fixes for a deadly poor state,

poorly run (with squandered human resources).
In that sense BMW is no different than our rice,
gold, canals, cotton, textiles, or phosphate. Only in

duration do they differ. I see those farmers
slathering rows with shovel loads of deep time's
rich fruit and by-product, buried millions of years,

and yes, springing forth fertility to pad bank
accounts, even pull a few upward from Hard-Luck
to Easy Street, but also perpetrate the Power-ball

dreams of the South Carolina poor, to catapult
hopes from Here (pork-n-beans and Spam) to There
(T-Bone) in one long stride, to strike it rich, move on.

RAY MCMANUS

Train-car wreck. Beulah Glover Photograph Collection, Accession no. 12239.62, Folder 6.
Courtesy of South Caroliniana Library, University of South Carolina, Columbia, S.C.

Pipeline

The car idles fast. The last one was totaled.
At the crossroads, teeth are thrown and go missing.
We keep our love in pillowcases and bang them on banks
when the radio plays sad songs because there's nothing

else to do. Out here nobody cares to see where bones
land, because this is the place to lose things, where rust
sleeps in pastures, where horses go to die. According
to the map, the route of egress stops somewhere

between backfill and setback, so we crash on the edge,
half in/half out, split by hard-cut and easement,
the product of not paying attention to the length
of ditches. And like the afternoons of so many

wasted days and all that is half buried, this is nothing
new, just a cut of it, the mess we leave behind.

JILLIAN WEISE

Train. Electric of Bob's. August 1951. Don Herd Photograph Collection, Reference no. 12499.984.

Train, Electric of Bob's

Up to a point, precision
the ability to change direction

Twice cites the mountain
as a major influence

Summers in the attic
Renovation and reverse loop

Sometimes breathed upon
heavily in the night

Trouble coupling, uncoupling
Nothing, my love, to deliver

Knows beyond warranty
the end of the track

Long-standing complaint
against the whistle

PAM DURBAN

Unidentified House—Iron banister. Marsh Photograph Collection, Folder 9883 15–33,
Accession number 9883–17. Courtesy of South Caroliniana Library,
University of South Carolina, Columbia, S.C.

The Cure

Sarah was a pilgrim and a stubborn girl, only child of Catherine and Edward, a prosperous Georgia cotton farmer. *Bull-headed,* her father called her, but proudly, fondly, in the eighteen years that passed between her birth and his death in 1910. Not even a year after, Sarah needed that strong will and her father's money, too. Just before her nineteenth birthday, her cough began, the bloody handkerchiefs started piling up on her bedside table, until her mother finally closed up the house and took her daughter away to find a cure.

Half a century earlier, she might have been sent to Dr. John Croghan's sanatorium deep in a limestone chamber in Mammoth Cave, down where the doctor believed his tubercular pilgrims were safe from the harmful solar influences. She was spared that experiment that ended one year later with most of the pilgrims dead and the sanatorium closed, the doctor himself dead a few years later, for while the solar influences could not touch Dr. Croghan's invalids, human error could, and did, like the one he made when he failed to realize how the thick smoke from cooking fires and torches would damage the lungs of his suffering flock.

By the time Sarah got sick it was a new century, and advances in scientific knowledge were driving the belief in the *solar influences* back into the shadows of ignorance and superstition where it belonged. Still, the tubercular pilgrims and their doctors believed that somewhere on this wide and ruthless earth, there was a kinder place where air, soil, elevation and light—the four conditions they were called—were so perfectly balanced they created a healing paradise. Not a new belief, certainly, not a faith that's easily shaken either, this belief in a place of harmony and healing or the miles and years we will travel to find it.

Two years earlier, Tucson, Arizona had looked promising, and the pilgrims flocked there. If they had the means, as Sarah and her mother did, they lived in a boarding house or sanatorium; the poorer invalids pitched their tents in the desert outside of town. In Tucson, the hot, dry air was good for Sarah, but the wind was bad. It blew almost constantly, carrying hawks and buzzards up into the blue, blue sky, spreading the smell of sage across the desert after rain, carrying, mostly, sand to blast paint from wood and scour Sarah's lungs. Finally, after a towering sandstorm hid the sun for hours, Sarah and Catherine fled to Sarnac Lake in upstate New York, where the air was as cool and clear as water and fragrant with balsam and cedar and Sarah sat in the sun on a stone terrace overlooking a quiet lake, trying to make the water's calm her own. Most sanatoriums were built on high ground then, to offer an inspiring view and encourage optimism.

At first, things were good for Sarah at Sarnac Lake. From the rising bell at 7:15 to lights out at 9:30, her days were filled with peace; her only job was to breathe and rest. For four months, she sat in the sun on the stone terrace behind the sanatorium, trying to achieve the absolute stillness that it was thought might save her. Her mother swooped in and out, bossed the help, blew kisses from the edge of the terrace, from across the room. They both knew it had to be this way. If her mother wanted to live, she had to keep her distance. Wherever they went, she rented a room in a house or hotel among the healthy companions of other sick travelers. She stayed close to her daughter, but not too close, wearing a gauze mask over her mouth and nose that she washed daily and dried in the sun.

During those first four peaceful months at Sarnac Lake, Sarah's cough grew more urgent. It clawed its way up from some deep place and wracked her for ten minutes or more, as though if she could cough long enough and hard enough she might cough up her sickness the way a cat coughs up a hair-ball onto a carpet. But the coughing freed nothing. Its only reason for being was to advance its own cause, and so, every day as Sarah sat on the terrace, and every night as she slept in her small, neat room, the branching tree of breath and life in her lungs dropped a few more leaves, the river of fibers carrying oxygen to every cell narrowed, stiffened and thinned.

Finally, after five months in that tranquil place, Catherine sent a telegram to Sarah's doctor in Atlanta. *Urgent.* She wrote. *Where now? Send word.* Their doctor

was not out of options yet; he hadn't given up hope, and he wouldn't allow them to give it up either.

He read all the current medical journals, and he'd recently come across several articles about a promising small town in the South Carolina sand hills. Through a series of telegrams and telephone calls across an unreliable long distance line, he sketched the town for Catherine. It was situated on the fall line, he told her, the shore of the ancient eastern ocean, on the brow of a hill close to the Savannah River but high enough to escape the heat and damp of the river bottom swamps. The four conditions were exquisitely balanced there. Getting there was easy, too, he said. No rough overland journey required, just swift passage on a steamboat down the east coast to Charleston (the ocean voyage itself believed to be restorative) then *quickly* onto a train that would carry them one hundred and twenty miles inland, to Aiken. "Listen carefully, Madam," he said. The word *quickly* was carefully chosen. They must not linger in Charleston, he said. No matter how tempted, they must resist the city's charms. "Lash yourself to the mast, dear lady," he said, playing to Catherine's knowledge of the classics. Bundle your daughter onto the first train, he advised, and flee the heavy air, the standing pools of brackish water, the stifling atmosphere of decay that hangs so heavy above that moldy old town.

They always did exactly what their doctor told them to do. They repeated his instructions like a prayer or a spell and followed them down to the last detail. "Go here," he said, and they went. As usual, there was an urgency about leaving one place and going to another, a sense of escape, as though they were fleeing a cresting wave. It was nearly August now, and Sarah could still pack her own suitcase, and wanted to, and did. Packing made her feel as though she still had a say in things. As long as she could fold, smooth, arrange her clothing in the suitcase, she wasn't just being swept along, helpless, like a twig on a fast-moving stream. Down the coast to Charleston they sailed, then they hurried onto the Aiken train, and, finally, they were no longer escaping, they were moving *toward* a new place.

They were the only passengers in the car on the Aiken train reserved for invalids. Her mother sat a few rows away from Sarah, keeping watch while Sarah dozed and dreamed that the branching tree of life in her lungs had sprouted new spring-green leaves. Between Sarah's naps, her mother read to her from an article the doctor had sent. Aiken, she read, was a land of pines and soft, dry air and sand so clean and white it looked like snow in the moonlight. Flocks of rich people wintered there, Catherine told her daughter, the *big rich,* she called them: Whitneys and Goodyears and Hitchcocks. Rich people and their handsome horses who came to town to play polo and ride behind a pack of hounds baying after a bag of fox scent dragged along the trails through a big tract of pine woods there. The deep sand was good for their horse's legs. Their company was good for one another and they prospered in Aiken, they thrived. In fact, Catherine read to her daughter, one sickly little rich girl was brought to Aiken to take the cure and now look at her—married to a wealthy horseman, surrounded by friends. It was a very good sign that the rich had chosen this place her mother said. The rich didn't go to shabby places, to places that disappointed or failed them.

The local population was congenial, refined, welcoming, her mother read. They operated hotels and boarding houses for the sick traveler, and a large contingent of good nurses and doctors stood ready to attend to an invalid's needs. A Dr. Geddings was mentioned. As a man of science, his belief in Aiken's healing climate was based on something firmer than hope. His theory was that of the four conditions, dryness was key, for in dry conditions, he wrote, the TB bacillus "appears to become inert, and, for the time being, harmless." Furthermore, he had discovered the secret of this life-giving dryness. "*The soil of Aiken,*" he wrote, "*is composed of loose sand, white on the surface, but of every conceivable hue as we pass through the different strata. The natural drainage resulting from the location of the town on the brow of a hill is materially facilitated by the great porosity of the soil, through which the water is rapidly filtered, so that even after a heavy fall of rain the invalid is seldom confined to the house for any considerable length of time. This is a feature of no little importance to those to whom 'every moment spent indoors is a moment lost.' This sandy soil is a good absorbent of moisture, and thus contributes to the dryness of the surrounding air.*"

Sarah breathed and listened. She liked to see her mother so animated, loved the greedy look that came over her face as she read about the rich people and the miraculous sand. It had been so long since she'd felt greedy for anything but quiet and rest. She looked back on greed the way she looked at her childhood, something that had happened to her long ago.

The train glided into Aiken as though it had reached the land in Sarah's dream. The sand was as white as promised, the pines as tall, the sky as blue. "What a fine little town," her mother said, walking up and down the platform where their suitcases had been unloaded. She breathed deeply as she walked, praised the air, the light. "Don't you feel better already?" she said. Sarah sat on her suitcase, fighting for breath, but she nodded and agreed.

At the invalid's boarding house and the hotel next door, they were looked after by colored people who fetched and carried, cooked and washed and hauled. Every week, the women stripped the linen from the invalid's beds. They collected the bloodstained, sputum-crusted handkerchiefs, the shirts, gowns and corsets and trundled the soiled loads by mule wagon to wash pots set up over fires near a local spring. Every month, the men dragged the rugs out of the hotels and boarding houses and beat them until the dust flew up and away. The men didn't get sick as often as the washer women. The dust that flew off of the rugs they beat was Dr. Geddings's dry, harmless dust, while TB thrived and swarmed in the steam that rose from the wash pots.

Sometimes the men made a contest of the rug-beating, or they competed to see who could eat the most watermelons at one sitting, and the rich men stood around and bet on the contests. The rich men would bet on anything. Which glass of milk a fly would land on. Which card would fall from the deck. Which woman would marry next. Her mother slipped into this world as smoothly as a hand slides into a soft leather glove. Every day, she twisted and pinned up her auburn hair in a different style, and men hovered around her where she sipped coffee at one of the small white tables set up on the brick terrace behind the hotel.

Most mornings, Sarah was the first invalid—the *guests* they were called, as though they'd been missed and invited there—to lean on Minnie or Annie or Bertha

Mae and make her slow way to the long back gallery that spanned the length of the boarding house and let herself be lowered into one of the reclining chairs there. It was early September when they got to Aiken, and sitting on the gallery with her face turned up to the thin sunlight of early autumn, Sarah felt herself thin and fade, too. At the hotel next door, the steps leading down from terrace to ground were lined with a white wrought iron handrail, its design a series of ornate medallions that looked to Sarah like chariot wheels, or some other fiery force, rolling toward glory.

Watching her mother and the other guests descend the brick steps between the beautiful railings and walk off down the sandy path that led away from the hotel, she felt that she was watching a procession in which she no longer walked. At first, it seemed a bitter injustice that something as heavy and motionless as iron could express the power and energy of motion, or that her mother should brighten as Sarah faded, as if *she* had been the one who'd been cured of whatever she'd been dying of before they came. But as September moved on, it began to seem that bitterness and injustice belonged to a world that she observed from a greater distance every day.

By the end of September, she felt as insubstantial as a ghost, and the gauzy feeling only left her when her mother came over from the hotel to say good-night. She did not seem glamorous then, or cured. With her hair down and her face scrubbed and plain, she looked like the mother Sarah had always known. "I love you," Catherine said from the doorway, and then she held her breath and waited for her daughter to throw back that same frayed lifeline of words, the one that people keep throwing to one another, even when there's no hope of rescue.

September became October, and in spite of the mornings on the terrace, the rest and quiet, the good food and the love, Sarah waned. Many nights, Catherine woke gasping for breath, and after the first wave of panic passed she welcomed the breathlessness because it brought her closer to Sarah. But she was strong-willed, too, and the next morning, she wouldn't let the fear stop her from getting out of bed, pinning up her hair and going out to find someone to save her daughter's life. Down the brick steps she went, along the sandy path, all her movements urgent, her footsteps quick. One day at Dr. Geddings's office she pushed ahead of others, demanded answers. Hearing her daughter's story, Dr. Geddings gave her a handsome, leather-bound book of his reflections in which he wrote that should the waves of the old eastern ocean crash upon this shore again, the forgiving sand would render the water harmless in the twinkling of an eye. "As we traverse this vale of tears," he wrote, "we will not fear, for our feet tread upon the substance of hope and salvation."

"Have faith, dear lady," he said as he ushered her out of his examining room. "Take heart."

Meanwhile, as October began, Sarah slept away the morning in her chair on the sunny gallery. All afternoon she slept in her narrow bed. Finally, on an unseasonably hot morning in early October, she did not wake up, and

after her mother came and sat for a long time beside her bed with her hands over her face, weeping and calling her name, she was carried down a flight of stairs at the side of the house and into to an alley where the undertaker's wagon waited.

What would she do now? Where would she go? How would she live? Catherine asked herself every day on her walk to the cemetery, and after a month had passed, an answer came to her and she knew that she wasn't going back to her late husband's house and cotton fields. To return without her daughter to the place they had left with such determination would be disheartening, an admission of defeat. Then one day in mid-November when she arrived at the cemetery with a pot of russet mums for Sarah's grave, she found one of the rich men from the hotel patio standing over a fresh grave next to Sarah's. His nephew, he said. Beloved boy. My daughter, she said. The light of my life.

That morning she walked back to the hotel, marveling at how quickly a bond can form between souls that have shared suffering, and she knew that they would meet again. Besides, a man had a way of looking at you that showed that he liked what he saw and wanted to see more. She would find a hairdresser to apply a rinse to mask the gray in her hair and make up her face to lighten the sadness so that he would be glad to see her again, and she would tell him that she planned to make her home in Aiken. She could not leave her daughter here alone, she would say, and that would be true, but not the whole truth, which almost never gets told because we always hold something back—maybe the best part—for later, so that the story never really ends.

All this time, out of loyalty to her late husband, she had worn her wedding ring, but back in her room on the day she met the rich man, she worked it off her finger and dropped it into the cut-glass dish on the dresser where she kept her smaller pieces of jewelry. The faint clink of the ring against the glass made her feel lighter, and she remembered another one of Dr. Geddings' reflections.

Drown this place, he wrote, swamp it, pour a bucket of blood out onto it, the sand would soon emerge from the flood, serene and untroubled. Maybe, she thought, her life could be like that sand, and in a few days, once the mark of the ring had disappeared, she would be free again to be courted and pursued.

CHARLENE SPEAREN

Ashley, Audrey—June 12, 1950, Belton, Infant in coffin and grave.
E. Don Herd Negative Collection, Reference no. 12499.45. Courtesy of
South Caroliniana Library, University of South Carolina, Columbia, S.C.

Crib Death

The Bible was raised the day she wore that satin gown
trimmed with lace from grandmother's wedding dress,

all a desire for perfection: the christening, her fingers,
toes, elbows, knees. Three days ago, I kissed her velvet

head, neatly untucked her arms, placed her on her
    tummy,
and turned the head toward the open door. Still
    happy, still

thinking, " A gift from God," I turned the lights out.
Now, I live inside the haze of a mournful muse,
    her cold

infant body, her face, like all babies, still makes real
the word "grace." Baby's breath flanks her tiny coffin,

and lilies, ruben and peace, perfume the air. "I am
    so sorry,"
one after the other mumbled like sacred prayers,
    march by,

a homage to the art of memory, and here and there,
a "God's will" dances like a brewing hurricane.
    A woman

brings a glass of water; her movement is like offering
communion. She does not know I have traveled to
    another world.

This place is better, and I can taste Olivia's sweetness,
    feel
the brush of her cheeks. Yet, somewhere, under my
    right thumbnail

I know I am still alive. King of Kings, Prince of Peace,
Son of God, Good Shepherd, why did you take
    my lamb?

MICHELE REESE

4 men with chickens. Harbison Agricultural College Collection, Accession no. 12525.43, Box 2.

Courtesy of South Caroliniana Library, University of South Carolina, Columbia, S.C.

Freedman's School

Surely, mama didn't buy me
this five piece suit to handle chickens.
She could have sent me out in the yard
in regular britches to do that—
not sent me off to some college
with big ol' brick buildings.
I'll listen to this teacher man
with his polished shoes and pressed pants.
I want to look as sharp as he does.
What else does a black man have?

Dog on horse. E. T. Start Photograph Collection, no. 57b, Sheet 3. Courtesy of
South Caroliniana Library, University of South Carolina, Columbia, S.C.

Humphrey

i   Do not worry that naps will make you lazy.
Porches were made for no other use but rest
and watching your neighbors at safe distances.

ii   I learned to keep an eye on my slippers and horse,
both of which he tried to make off with
when I was reading a novel in bed.

iii   Descendant of wolves and the tops of mountains,
he perches on pillows, the wingback chair,
anyone's lap.

iv   My father recites him the Boy Scout Law:
Trustworthy, loyal, helpful, friendly, courteous,
kind, obedient, cheerful, thrifty, brave, clean,
and reverent.

v   Eating the insides of things
is the only way to know

vi   I once bit a friend's cheek when she stole my chair
at nearly the same age as he is now.

vii Hold a small stone in your mouth
and think of nothing but this
stone and this mouth

GEORGE SINGLETON

Entrekin, Bill— (5) Negatives, Photographs of family. E. Don Herd Negative Collection, Reference no.

12499.360. Courtesy of South Caroliniana Library, University of South Carolina, Columbia, S.C.

Calling

Dear Fellow Devoted Christian Family Members and Devout Christian Friends:

To say the least, God has blessed the Entrekin family manifold this year, and we are grateful and amazed at His provisions. And utter surprises! How would we have known that we would be embarking on mission journeys that took us to three continents in this, Our Early Middle Age? (Unless He wants us to live to be 120, which would make us in our First Fourth Age!) (Or maybe 300 years, which would make this our One-Tenth Age!) (Quick test: Who lived to be 300 years old in the Old Testament? Answer: Just about everybody. Except for Abel!)

As all of you know, Bill always wondered why he lost interest in studying to be a veterinarian in college. And then he lost interest in being a doctor, and then in being an accountant. After quitting college, he oftentimes brooded over being "lost in a sea of self-doubt." And then he got that part-time job at the pharmacy, which got him interested in eyewear, which got God to direct him to optician's school for his associate's degree, which got him a job right away at Hub City Optical, next to Hub City Knife and Gun. In case you're wondering, Bill's coworkers were some of the most advanced and skilled in the country, no matter what anyone says. They had to be! Think of all the times people have been to the knife and gun place and accidentally got struck in the eye, and had to go immediately over to Hub City Optical for a specialized patch. Next thing you know, they're getting along fine with someone like Bill, and then they're buying eyeglasses.

I'm getting ahead of myself. The Entrekin family is here to tell you about places where you can get your eyewear for free, in a way.

Anyway, God spoke with Bill back in January, and He said, "Bill, you need to take your expertise to some of the poorer countries of the universe and help them out." Bill woke up one morning and told me about God's advice, and I believed him (and Him!) right away. It was the look in Bill's eye that told me he wasn't messing with me. As a matter of fact, Little Billy had the look in both his eyes! One thing about an optician's wife, you learn to keep track of your husband's eye, and your son's.

So we talked to our preacher, who got us in touch with the Baptist Eye Mission International organization, and the next thing you know me and Bill and Little Billy and I were on a plane to Ethiopia!

Ethiopia is a terrible poor country. It's next to Kenya. It would break your heart. It's next to Sudan. There's that other country down there touching the border, too, but I don't know how to pronounce it. We got to the capital city of Addis Ababa, and the good fine people of Baptist Eye got us on a bus to go down to the lowlands. We got there all right, for the most part. I forget how long it took us—the bus kept breaking down, and these soldiers kept showing up—but I know that for something like four days and nights we only ate something called "fit-fit." There's a reason why it's called "fit-fit"—after four days, you'll have a fit from eating it!

It's bread and yogurt, I guess would be the best way to describe it.

When we finally got to where we were going, and knowing that God was with us the entire way, Bill and I felt both relieved and summoned.

But how sad! Sometimes I think we forget everything we had there in the South Carolina. I know this will be hard to believe, but the reason why these little lowland Ethiopian children had bad eyesight was because—and I know this will be hard to believe—we came across a little village where no one had ears! It's true! They couldn't wear glasses if they wanted to!

Then at another village there was a leper colony. Little Billy just stared and stared at everyone and I think he was afraid, since I'd shown him Bible picture book cartoons and heard stories about lepers. Luckily, God spoke to Bill again and told him it was all right for us to move on to the next village. When we got there—by this time we'd eaten something called "hilbet" which was African for "refried beans"—the children all had ears, and weren't oozing from leprosy sores.

Did I mention that all this time we had to lug around something like 12,000 pairs of used eyeglasses in trunks and boxes?

Okay, so in the third village everything looked like it's what God had in mind for us. Bill gave the children some kind of eye test. We had an interpreter who talked to the local people. It sounded like they spoke in tongues perfectly! All these children put on their glasses, and before you know it some people came out of the woodwork and starting killing the children! They said that the children had become demonized, according to our interpreter.

I'm not sure what else went on there. I told Bill that God spoke to me and told us to take cover. Bill took off his glasses, and told me to take off mine and the ones that we had Little Billy wearing. Bill said for all of us to throw them into this giant cesspool there in the village where people got their drinking water, washed clothes, and used the bathroom. We did as instructed, and Little Billy didn't either laugh or cry about the change. He's the most wonderful child a mother could ask for!

So we were in Ethiopia for about two weeks, hoping for a long-term mission opportunity, but the Lord did not affirm a call.

We didn't hardly get settled back at home when God spoke to Bill again, and told him to contact the Baptist Eye People and see if they had a mission opportunity in Mexico, and this time He got real specific: the Lord told Bill that there were little Jewish children in Mexico who needed to hear our testimonials, and get new eyewear also.

So we got everything together and took off for what ended up being a gigantic trash dump on the outskirts of Mexico City. If Jews are the Chosen People, I don't understand why they'd choose this place to live, ha ha!

Anyway, we used this opportunity to have Little Billy learn the foreign language "Spanish," or at least be around it all the time. Do you know that Dear Abby once wrote that the words "Good" and "God" are very close in sound and spelling for a reason? That's true. It's true that she wrote it, and it's the Truth. In Mexico, the word for "Good" is "Bueno," and the word for "God" is "Dios." Those words don't sound so close together, if you ask me. "Dios" only needs one letter taken out and another added in to make the word "Dies." So I stopped the Spanish lessons immediately. It would be a different story if the word for "Good" was "Bueno" and the word for "God" was "Bruno."

The filth in a Mexican landfill! There were people out there—Jews and non-Jews alike, but not good Christians—digging around for bites of thrown away tacos and whatnot. It would break your heart. We met one little brother and sister who couldn't find something. They kept pointing, and calling out. I don't know where are interpreter ran off to. Bill reached into his backpack and pulled a pair of used eyeglasses for the little boy to try on so maybe he could recognize his parents out of all the bent-over Mexicans looking for dump food, but while he did that the little girl took off with all the other eyeglasses. You should've seen her run! Now I know why it's so easy for them to get across our borders without getting caught! I bet it didn't take her two seconds to cross over what may or may not have been a pile of dead cows, a bunch of scattered sombreros, and some of those little cars like they drive in France.

Bill said to me, "Sandy, where's Little Guillermo?" We had started calling him that because, you know, even though he wasn't but a toddler, we thought it might make him feel more accepted in a hostile, strange land.

I said, "What?" I guess I had set him down on a clean spot in the dump, and he just crawled off!

All of y'all without sin can blame me for what happened next. I went running in a couple directions, and then I tripped over something, and I landed on Little Billy and—of course!—he poked his eye on some kind of piece of a grocery shopping cart. I blame myself. But y'all know Bill—he took control of the situation, and got all us back to the hotel in order to call up a "el doctor."

Little Billy was fine. The doctor said he might "el squinto" for a while, but that he'd be "bueno" overall. But then we got to the motel afterwards a few hours later, only to find out that someone had broken into our room and stolen all of our used eyeglasses!

It was at this moment that the Lord did not affirm a longer call to Mexico.

But we had an eventful, God-fearing time. Looking back, it was a test for the Entrekin family.

We got back home, and Bill took back his shift at the Hub City Opticians for three years, three months, and three days. I know that y'all are probably wondering, Where did God ask Bill to take the Entrekin family next? Did He ask them to help the little children of Brazil or Russia, of Norway or Pakistan, of Australia or Sweden? If you've been paying attention, y'all know that I mentioned three continents. Where could the Entrekins have gone for the Trinity of Mission Trips?

God did not come down to Bill for the third mission trip sponsored by Baptist Eye. He was serious this time: He came to Little Billy. You should've seen the morning when he came down for breakfast to tell us their news!

Little Billy started up with, "I had dream, I had dream!"

And I go, "Was it a good dream?"

And Billy goes, "Yes ma'am. It was a glorious dream that involved strange women and people who were either ecstatic or downtrodden."

And then both Bill and I said, "Where did you learn words like that? Who wants to say Grace?"

And then Little Billy goes, "Daddy, what was it like when God came down to tell you that the Entrekin family needed to go to Ethiopia?"

And then Bill goes, "Children should be seen, not heard."

Well, Little Billy looked at us with his mouth open wide, kind of like those leper people do in those Bible picture books we got our pediatrician to tell us where to order. Bill said, "Did God come down and talk to you in your dreams?" He said, "God told me we need to get another couch, Sandy. I meant to tell you that."

Little Billy said, "I think." He went, "I know He told me where we should go."

The suspense about killed me. I remember saying out loud there at the breakfast table, "Sandy, you're going to die from the suspense." Where would we be sent next by His Divine Hand?

"Reno, Nevada!" Little Billy yelled out. I swear that's what he yelled out! Four years old! How could he know, without God's Divine Hand and Mouth?

Now, I know that some of the more skeptical Christians in our extended network might think, "No way!"

But if Little Billy really wanted to make up something, wouldn't he have said "Las Vegas"? Wouldn't he have gotten the idea from one of those secular children he witnesses to in the neighborhood?

Bill said, "The Lord knows what's for the best. That only makes sense! People can't see very well from staring at slot machines twenty-two hours out of every day. And it'll give us the opportunity not only to help their physical visions, but help their spiritual visions through our testimonials and Christian guidance."

The people at Baptist Eye were skeptical, I must say, but when Bill chimed in that he too had had the affirmation from God, they couldn't turn down our request. Later on I said, "Bill, you didn't have the vision from the Lord like Little Billy did."

He said, "Sandy, let me tell you what I learned on about the first day of Optician's School—it's okay to fib a little bit for the Greater Good."

Maybe I shouldn't be telling tales on my husband in this, the Holiday Season. But I believe with all my heart that he was right!

Reno, Nevada, is known as "The Biggest Little City in the World." I don't know about that. What does that even mean? For me personally, the Biggest Little City in the World would be Bethlehem.

Anyway—and I know that I have to wrap up this Christmas letter some time soon so all of y'all have time to do some shopping!—we got there with our truckload of free glasses. Bill found out that a bunch of the showgirls and hostesses had bad vision and needed extra special time with him, trying on pair after pair of eyeglasses before one gave them good vision. I thought it was going to be all about the older people and tourists going half-blind on those newfangled one-armed bandits, but that wasn't the case.

Me, I found out that the Lord wanted me to tithe more per Sunday, so He had me accidentally find a twenty dollar bill on the floor of our hotel lobby, take it into the casino, have it changed to silver dollars, and start sticking them in a machine—I don't even remember doing any of this, but Bill said it was like watching an old zombie movie—and then win the jackpot!

I swear that I didn't even know how to play! I didn't even know the rules! The next thing you know, this light went off flashing on top of my machine, and this little tiny woman barely wearing any clothes at all came up, and I had to grab some buckets to hold all the silver dollars. Bill took one look at her and said, "I see that you're squinting quite a bit." To me he said, "God is saying that you have found your niche, and that you should keep winning sinful money in order to put it to good use." To the woman he said, "Come up to my room and I'll fit you."

The Baptist Eye People are extremely happy and proud of Bill's work here. And God is, too. Bill feels called to a full time mission here. So do I. So does Little Billy, who, by the way, says he's embarrassed that I'm sending out this family picture from when he was a baby. Kids! But when have we had time to take new family portraits?!

But as y'all know, there's no telling if and when the Lord asks that we pick up and move to somewhere else, somewhere far off, like Monte Carlo, or the Bahamas.

But let it be known that the Entrekin Family is forever blessed. We hope to come back home soon in order to visit. We hope so. Bill thinks he might should get a part-time position at the local Biggest Little City in the World Eyewear. Me, I have to admit that I feel as though I've let the Lord down. I've been on a losing streak, which means I can't tithe. Why would God ask me to play the machines in order to help out His Ministry, then have me go on such an unlucky streak?

I can't make sense out of it, either. The older I get, the less I can make sense out of anything, I'm afraid. I need to talk to Bill about this certain backsliding self-doubt I feel coming on, but I don't see him as much as I'd like. He's busy, and I don't want to bother him with my little problems. Good strong Christian families need to remember that we're here for reasons we can't always understand. My quandaries (sp?) mean nothing, in the overall scheme of things. "This, too, shall pass," as I've always learned to say.

Happy Holidays! —
Sandy

RICHARD GARCIA

House where Union officers were confined under fire, Broad St. Stereographic Views of South Carolina, Call Number 12612. Courtesy of South Caroliniana Library, University of South Carolina, Columbia, S.C.

Postcard from a
Civil War Reenactment

Had breakfast at the Sweet Shop. A placard at the entrance: *Arms and legs were thrown out the second story window. A wagon waited below to receive them.* Last night, I slept at the college. The hallways were lined with empty cots. As was the library, City Hall, the Church of the Redeemer, even the cemetery was lined with cots. I thought there would be formations, marching in step, uniforms, and loud but harmless explosions. I saw an old man wandering through an alley who looked like Walt Whitman. Sometimes he would crouch down close to the ground. He seemed to be speaking to someone. 5:30 AM, mist low over the fields. I had expected reveille but it was silent. Except for one mockingbird that was imitating the songs of different birds, hoping one would answer, revealing the location of its nest.

DANIEL NATHAN TERRY

Charleston—Residence—Drayton Hall and 2 side buildings. George LaGrange Cook Photograph Collection, Box 3;
Temporary num. 55. Courtesy of South Caroliniana Library, University of South Carolina, Columbia, S.C.

Possession

DRAYTON HALL (BUILT C. 1740), CHARLESTON, SOUTH CAROLINA

Listen— the tribe, our mind, this collective
sighing in the heart of the house, song of conversion,
of reclamation. Etiwan and African, builders, kings

and queens, witches, warriors, mothers, ghosts
whispering the ancient music in your attic dreams
while you twisted in basement sleep. Time dissolves

these beams, the plaster stars above your head,
the sugared wood within this hall will be returned to us,
to those bones in the earth who tended and shaped

these rooms, who raised this palace of clay and the stone
of your desire to possess this land. In death, we riddled,
tunneled, burrowed deep beneath the foundation,

deep into the riverbed. Deep and settled in.
Live your short life. Pretend you own this place,
while you pace its empty space. We can wait.

Day will come when you will want to forget
your great house and the hands of mud that pull
    it down.
And you will want to crawl from home

into the tangled sprawl of some live oak,
where there is a quiet nook in a forgiving limb
thick with moss and shadow, decay and resurrection

fern. And you will envy whatever creature, however
    small,
however insignificant, that can call this quiet green
and black pocket the whole of the world.

JANNA MCMAHAN

Calm before the storm—white swans at Brookgreen. Beulah Glover Photograph Collection,
Accession no. 12239.78, Folder 9. Courtesy of South Caroliniana Library,
University of South Carolina, Columbia, S.C.

The Curator

Harold Block was a curator of the most curious sort. He wasn't a people person and had no desire to pontificate about his shows. He rather enjoyed writing catalogs, but he loathed giving gallery lectures. But he had no choice in the matter. All exhibitions had to have an educational component, particularly in a small museum at a second tier university.

The curator knew why he chose each piece that went into an exhibition, but often he found it difficult to explain his selections to others. It was always easier when there was a significant historical context to an item. People seemed to take history as an unassailable indicator of value. Why of course it's in the show; it's historical! In past-obsessed South Carolina face jugs were always welcome, as were drippy watercolors and daguerreotypes of ancestral types.

He wrote brochures and descriptive placards. Sometimes catalogs were needed for larger shows curated in-house. He loved the research, the contemplation, the physical gallery time. His staff painted the walls a new color with each show. Then they spent days placing hangers, cleaning vitrines and positioning stanchions. He enjoyed all the physical effort required to present a show, the careful displaying of each work of art. But then he had to face the public.

While the curator hated giving gallery talks, what he dreaded most were opening-night receptions. At these events his suit seemed tighter than usual on his ample frame; his tie throttled his breathing. Sometimes he sneaked away to his office where he sipped the caterer's wine and listened to the hum of conversation overhead. More often he ended up in the men's room where he splashed water on his flushed face and combed the remaining strands of his hair back into place with damp fingers.

The museum director usually rapped on the door to check on him when he had gone missing too long.

"Harold?" she would call through the frosted glass. "Are you okay in there?" Eventually he had no choice but to return to the party.

The curator hated fielding questions from people as they chewed their mini-quiche and blanched vegetables. He went out of his way to dodge the rich, entitled patrons who droned on about the art they saw on their last trip abroad. Even worse were the poorly educated ones who babbled on about objects they knew nothing about.

Then there were the older patrons who yelled and spoke so slowly that Harold felt compelled to finish their sentences. At least the younger crowd left him alone; they came only for the free brie and booze.

The curator was always relieved when opening nights were over and he could fade back into the recesses of the stacks and racks that held the collection. Those days he was happiest alone with his beloved objects.

It was on such a contemplative afternoon in the dead of winter, when the light died early and cold crept into his basement office that the oddest thing happened. He had propped a collection of small historic photographs along the walls around his office. He'd studied each with a photography loop looking for details that the casual gallery visitor might miss. He needed a singular idea useful for connecting the images that would supply a theme for the show.

The photographs had been donated to the museum from the estate of a wealthy alumnus who had died at the astounding age of 106. The volume of the woman's collection had been overwhelming. It had taken the curator nearly three months to pull a core group of images that he could arrange into a coherent exhibition. And still there were dozens of boxes that he hadn't the time, nor the inclination, to open.

The museum's director had been most specific in her direction when the curator had told her that there was absolutely nothing remarkable about the collection of old photos. She had assured him that if he looked hard enough that he would indeed find the quality he sought; he had only to keep in mind the $200,000 the museum would receive from the estate once the exhibition was

up. Money was often the real theme behind exhibitions in a struggling museum.

The images were grainy and sepia. The curator turned each curl of thick photo paper over to read faded penciled notes scrawled in a florid hand. Most of the batch he had been examining that day were circa 1935–45. One in particular, an image of three white swans floating on a pond, had caught his attention. It was unusual for amateur photographers to try their hand at landscapes, but this lady had been ahead of her time.

Beulah Manning had photographed the usual people and houses and cars, but she had also had an eye for the lone slave descendent framed in the doorway of a ramshackle hut at the marshy edges of the sea. She'd captured abandoned boats, low-slung and weathered in the tangled flora of an inland waterway and beach houses that had lost their grandeur and loomed hollow and forlorn. Time had tarnished the familiar and he loved the otherworldly feeling of the photos, how they documented and obscured at the same time. But her images had a touch of melancholy that made him uneasy.

The swans were the only animals he'd discovered in the collection. Slightly fuzzy, obviously on the move when the shutter engaged, they were distant in the frame. A spit of land extended into the pond and at one point the curator thought he saw a person there where the camera had caught the memory of movement. But on inspection with a loop he found no ghostly outline, no streaks to indicate a person out of time with shutter speed.

He scanned the framed images and again felt drawn to the swans. Had he missed something? Was that a face he saw peeking from the depths of the tree cover? He picked up the piece and studied it. Maybe, just maybe there was a face. He laid it flat on his desk, focused light and ran his loop over the background of the image.

All he saw were shadows. He moved the loop around the photo slowly bringing different sections out in bulging detail. He could have sworn that there had been a face. Before he had thought it was the form of someone standing near the water's edge. This time it was a face. He knew it had been there, watching. Was that somebody watching the swans or the photographer?

A tremor of trepidation tickled his spine and he pushed the photo away.

He had the horrible feeling that perhaps he was the one being watched. He grabbed the framed image and set it back on the floor. This time he turned it to the wall.

Over the next week the curator oversaw the installation of the historic photograph collection. He had titled the show, "Visual Language of the Lowcountry: From the Collection of Miss Beulah Manning, 1927–1955." The show included nearly a hundred images. He'd chosen to hang the swans in a corner he rarely had reason to pass. It wasn't next to the bathrooms and certainly not where he would see it on his way to his office. Still, he couldn't shake the feeling of being observed.

The opening night reception was more gray than usual. There were plenty of canes and walkers. One ancient matron in a wheelchair oddly resembled the photo of Beulah Manning that accompanied the biography panel at the gallery's entrance. She was elegantly dressed with a precious antique cameo at her throat. Another woman, who was herself in her seventies and also well appointed and bejeweled, maneuvered the wheelchair through the crowd. They were coming toward him. The museum director hovered around them.

"Harold," the director said. "I'd like you to meet Mrs. Betty Pinckney. She's Mrs. Manning's sister. And this is her niece, Ann."

The older woman extended her hand, but was unable to raise her gaze to meet the curator's eyes. She turned her head to the side and indicated that she was ready to listen by tapping her ear.

"It's so nice to see you," the curator said. "Mrs. Pinckney, what do you think of the exhibition?"

"She can't answer you," her niece said. "She's about stone deaf and dementia has finally gotten a hold on her. Don't worry about trying to carry on a conversation. And you can call her Miss Betty. Everybody does."

This candor stunned the curator, but he was grateful not to have to make small talk.

The old woman pointed and their gaze followed.

"She wants to look at some of the pictures," the niece said. "But they're so high on the wall. Can you take one down so she can see?"

It was unorthodox to remove a piece from the wall, particularly during an opening, but the director nodded.

The curator shrugged. "Sure. Why not?"

The niece followed as he made his was through the crowd to an image of three people in front of a shiny new Packard. He thought an image of people might be likely to elicit a response if anyone touched the old woman's memory. He bent down and placed the frame in her lap. She focused and then quickly waved the offering away.

"No," Miss Betty said distinctly.

The niece shrugged. "Try another?"

"I thought perhaps seeing people she might recognize would appeal."

"You never know what is going to get her attention. She likes animals. You have anything with animals?"

"Not much. Just one with a few swans in the background, but they're small and faded. I doubt she could see them."

"It's worth a try."

The curator removed the picture of the swans and offered it for inspection.

It took a moment for her to focus. Suddenly, with hands like talons she grasped the image and pulled it close.

"There they are," she said. "There!" She tapped the glass with a skeletal finger.

"Who Aunt Betty? Who're you talking about? There's nobody in that photo."

"There!" she insisted. "There they are. There!"

The niece looked at the curator with a quizzical expression. "She thinks she sees something, I guess."

"Miss Betty," the curator said. "What do you see?"

"They're there. Right there."

"Who? Who's there?"

"Don't worry about it," the niece said. "She's probably just having a moment. She comes and goes."

It was likely that the woman's reaction was only fantasy, but perhaps, like him, she saw something no one else could see.

"There was no identification on the back of this image," he said to the niece. "Do you know where this pond is located?"

"I can't be completely sure, but it could be the one on our family farm."

"How nice. A family farm. Does your family still own it?"

"A cousin does. I mean if that actually is the same place. You know a waterline can change over the years. We weren't allowed to play there when we were young. My grandmother was afraid we'd drown. If it is our pond it dried up years ago. My great-uncle filled it in the rest of the way. He was afraid it would breed mosquitoes."

After the caterers had cleared out and all the doors were locked, the curator made his way back to his office, the presence of the strange photo pressing on him. He sipped a glass of wine and contemplated the holdings room where the rest of the Manning photograph collection lived. The family would come to collect the lot in a few weeks when the exhibition came down.

His hunch was baseless, but something told him that he had to keep looking. Maybe he would unearth a clue that would prove the old woman was recalling something specific. Perhaps he would find another image at the pond where there was a wonderful family picnic on a sunny day. It would be his good deed to give her a snapshot of a long-ago afternoon with family when she was young. Perhaps it would spur the family to a larger donation.

He would do it fast. He didn't have days to waste this time. He didn't bother with the white curatorial gloves. Nobody would know. Nobody would care.

He took the first box of photos to the light table and began to sift through them. There were bundles and bundles of photos bound with dry rubber bands that crumbled at his touch. They were all in the same vein—people, houses, cars, cotton fields and shrimping boats. Most of the people were serious, unsmiling, dour even. Only the children had an untroubled look about them.

Sometime around four in the morning, with his neck aching and his eyes stinging he hauled the last carton of photos to the table. Certain that his search had been futile, he upturned the contents and from the bottom tumbled a cigar box. An exotic Cuban woman on the golden label smiled at him. The box was bound by unbroken tape. He took an artist's knife and sawed his way through the yellowed binding.

The top cracked and fell away from the box when he opened it. Inside were more photographs, all turned facedown. He gingerly slid them into his hand, turned them upright and caught his breath.

Dead babies. Newborns, although a couple were likely a few months old. He fanned them apart on the table, a dozen in all, but there were two and three angles of each child. Their tiny eyes were closed. None were dressed in the usual funeral finery of the time, no white lace or baby bonnets. These postmortem children were either nude or wrapped in blankets. None were in bassinets or miniature caskets.

Their faces were distorted and large, their limbs foreshortened and twisted. The curator wondered if they had downs syndrome or dwarfism or something much worse. One's mouth was open as if it had died mid-scream. There were no adults in the photos, no grieving mothers holding their wasted prizes. The images were cold, documentation only. He flipped each one over looking for any type of description. There was nothing. No date. No location. No name.

Had Beulah Manning taken these? Had she been called to the homes of her neighbors to document the stillborn and young dead of bereaved parents? Had this been a hobby or a profession for which she was paid?

The curator was suddenly exhausted and so terribly sad for the pallid, limp children in his hands. He suspected they weren't just memories hidden away in a box. They were a secret.

There was a time when death was closer to home. When people laid their dead in the parlor and neighbors came to pay their respect. Often photographers were called in to take images that were kept as mementos and sent to relatives who could not attend the ceremony. But these images of abnormal dead infants were beyond the customs of those days.

The curator was no stranger to historical photographs of open caskets and propped up corpses. An idea for an exhibition came to him. People were always interested in the macabre. That would be a show he could sell. He would have to create a separate room for these particular shots with signs that warned people of their disturbing nature, but no doubt attendance would pick up.

He would have to do research. Find out if birth certificates were issued. He knew where to start. He would begin with Miss Betty. Her niece said her focus waned, but at times she had clarity of thought. Without her, he could flounder for weeks looking for answers. If only she would awaken from old age long enough to point him in the right direction.

The curator arrived at the assisted-living facility while breakfast was being cleared. The old woman's niece had said he was welcome to visit her aunt, but she hadn't offered to meet him. He had been vague when he spoke of finding other photos that her aunt might recognize.

A nurse in pink scrubs showed him to the room. It was a nicely appointed private room with hardwood floors and brass doorknobs. The old woman was near the window in her rolling chair. She was backlit against the sunlight outside and a corona of wispy colorless hair glowed around her face. She watched a small bird in a tree outside. A sound machine pumped a rumble of ocean waves into the room.

"She like that ocean thing," the nurse said. "Reminds her of growing up at the beach."

"If I'd known I would have brought her some shells," the curator said.

The nurse shrugged. "She might come to. You can give it a try. Just yank that cord if you need me." And she was gone.

He positioned a chair close to the window too.

"Miss Betty?" he said. No response.

He tried a little louder. "Miss Betty, do you remember me? I'm Harold Block, the curator from the museum yesterday."

It took a moment for her to realize someone had called her name. She touched her hearing aid to make sure it was working, then she turned toward him and her eyes opened wide. She reached forward and laid a hand against his cheek. A look of love came over her and he realized that she must think him someone else.

He pulled the picture of the swans from his satchel. He had left a note when he took the photo from the museum so his staff wouldn't panic when it came up

missing. He placed it on her lap. Again she took a moment to focus. She ran her fingers over the glass.

"Miss Betty, is this your home?"

Her eyes played across the image.

"Is that your pond? Did your family swim here? Did you have a picnic?"

Her gaze fell to the window and then returned to the image.

"There they are," she said. A soft smile played across her face.

"Who Miss Betty? Your family? Your sister, Miss Beulah?"

She drifted off again and he realized that he wasn't going to get much more information than he had the night before. No need to prolong the situation.

From the depths of his satchel he pulled the cigar box. She reached forward to take it as if she expected it to be a present. He hesitated. Seeing all the images at once had startled him. Perhaps he needed to reveal them slowly for her.

"Here, I'll show you," he said. "Have you ever seen this photo before?" He held an image forward, one that wasn't quite as grotesque as some.

Her eyes went wide. A moan started low in her throat and came crawling up out of her. She slapped a wrinkled hand over her mouth and suppressed a sob. Her bloodshot eyes filled with tears.

"I'm sorry. I'm so sorry, Miss Betty. I'll put it away. I didn't mean to upset you."

"No." She put out her hand and he gently laid the photo in her palm. As she studied the contorted baby, tears pooled in her eyes and spilled onto her hollow cheeks.

"So many babies," she whispered.

"Do you know this baby?"

She didn't reply.

"What about this one?" He held up another photo for her to see.

She reached for them all and tears flowed.

"You know them?"

Her voice was suddenly dreamy and childlike.

"Grandfather baptized them . . . in the pond."

"He was a preacher?"

She shook her head. No.

"Who are these children?"

She looked directly at him. "Why, they're our babies, of course."

"Whose?"

"Our house girl's. Our maid's girl, Mandy. She was simple. All those babies, Grandfather said they were simple too."

Someone wailed in the hall, a low, mournful sound. The curator jumped and goose flesh crawled his arms. He cleared a nervous rattle from his throat.

"Why would your sister take these photos?"

"She didn't. Momma did. Momma took them. She said to remember. She said . . . she said so Grandfather would leave us alone."

"Leave who alone?"

"Us girls."

"You and your sister Beulah?"

She nodded.

Did it work? the curator wondered. She had said, "Our babies." Had their mother been successful in sacrificing the maid's daughter in order to save her own? Had time changed the story in the old woman's mind? Or was this selective memory at play?

"Miss Betty. What happened to the babies?"

"God took them."

"I know, but what happened to their little bodies?"

She pointed to the framed image on the floor.

"There they are."

Realization washed him.

"They're in the water," he said.

She leaned forward and motioned for him to come near. He bent close to her.

"They waited," she whispered, her breath warm in his ear. "They waited to be buried. Momma wanted to bury them, but Grandfather said no. So they waited."

And they watched from the depths of their murky grave, he thought. *They waited and they watched.*

"Is that why your uncle filled in the pond?" he asked, but the old woman's mind had turned away from him.

Her attention shifted to the sunny window where her rheumy eyes followed a wren flitting from branch to branch in a winter-barren tree. The bird's beak opened and its throat flared in song, but its sweet sound was drowned in a crash of ocean waves.

Impressions

WILLIAM WRIGHT

Beach Houses. Beulah Glover Photograph Collection, Accession no. 12239.30, Folder 3.
Courtesy of South Caroliniana Library, University of South Carolina, Columbia, S.C.

Edisto Gothic

1.

Once, when the scapular angles of trees made their exit
and let salt eat the edges of the earth away, a house was built
before so many behind the dune-shadows of Edisto Island's coast.
In the image of this house, the eye sees no bleakness, the cloud like smoke rising
from the chimney's tip. No warning of water's encroachment,
the Atlantic gasping behind the image's making, broken forms
of the ocean's otherworld glittering in oyster shards, melampus,
a clump of seaweed. Here are many childhoods, including
my own: a portrait of distance, the past refracted
through the windows that hold the light for good.

2.

I walk into my love of an old image, a past that could never be
mine, feeling my muscles sing their cycles, suspended between
the heat of a Carolina noon and the sand that scalds, then steams,
my bare soles.

Elements keep shattering this clarity. The dark creeps in from the west.
Dusk lures walkers with their lanterns until
wind picks up and stings their skin, pulls them back in.

The silhouette of a man emerges suddenly, walks beside me and waves.
His jacket snaps behind him like a cape. I wave back.
I cannot see his face.

3.
It is a difficult time to know the world. It is a difficult time
to winnow the old beach house that sits so still, so provisional.

And even kindness makes no difference to the forms that pulse
the tides, the blood centered in its rhythm.

This night, the moon rises somewhere, horn or whole or wholly
new, blasts the waters with as much light as it will give.

SAMUEL AMADON

Charleston—Church—Enston Home Chapel—Interior, 900 King St. George LaGrange Cook Photograph Collection, Box 2; Temporary num. 22. Courtesy of South Caroliniana Library, University of South Carolina, Columbia, S.C.

Poem for Susan Lewis

I don't know where Spencer is.
I mean I don't know where I am.
I have a picture of a church,
three sections of light. Or a rope

line. Two little dogs on it, but one at
a time. I'm in South Carolina,
with purple flowers under my sill.
Or I'm on Kenyon Street, eating

pretzels in your pantry, thank you
for the seltzer, thank you for
pulling into the breakdown lane,
thank you for everything. We're

all going to the store, and I keep
walking into Spencer, and he
doesn't like it. He's crying about
it, and it's my fault. You talk

to him, but you don't say
a thing about me. Three sections
of light. One's bigger
than the others. None of this fits

together, and I have a better way
to make it fit, but
I'm not going to do that.
Let's say I'm a teacher. Like you.

Like Spencer. Let's put the three
of us in a room. We'll tell
these people how we don't know
how to live, but do

anyway. Let's put me on the base
of the bathtub, a pile of wrenches,
and the hot water filling up. Let's
put Spencer in the garage, with

a bag of cigarettes. Or spray paint.
Let's walk the dog, and let's watch
our step. I have a picture
of a church, three sections of light.

You be the big one. Spencer and I
can be the other two. We'll stay.
We'll have this be worth something,
even though it doesn't have to be.

JOHN MARK SIBLEY-JONES

Untitled Photograph. E. E. Burson Photograph Collection, Print no. 146, Folder 10.

Courtesy of South Caroliniana Library, University of South Carolina, Columbia, S.C.

It's Time You Know Your People

My father climbed into the attic on the day he lost his job. On the last rung of the ladder, he looked down at us—Mom, Emma, and me—and shook his finger. "Don't even think of coming up here. I need to be alone." Then he took the last step and disappeared as he pulled up the door.

I knew he kept his father's old Army pistol up there, but it was a topic we never discussed. Mom hated guns. She gave in only because it was an heirloom. I could tell from the look on her face as she stared up at the attic door that she was wondering whether she'd hidden it well enough.

"Milt," she called up to him. "Milt? Can you hear me? Are you all right? We'll find another job, honey. The children and I need you."

"Take the children for a walk, Tess. Please." His voice was distant. Not like a voice from behind a closed attic door. Different. A voice from a deep cave. A voice from the bottom of a well.

Mom hesitated. Then she looked at Emma and me, bit her lower lip, and ushered us outside. We walked three blocks to the empty school playground. I straddled the see-saw, sought the balance between ground and air, and after a few moments gave up and sat in the sand.

Mom pushed Emma in the baby swing. Jaw clenched. Eyes closed once she established the rhythm of the swing as it swept skyward, paused at the apex, and arced back toward her. Each time the seat returned to her open hand and pushed against it, her head bobbed like it was loosely attached to her neck.

It seemed like hours before she opened her eyes and looked at me. Her desperate gaze made my stomach hurt. I understood that she was asking of me something she'd never asked before: *Be strong. Help me.* I probably didn't think it at the time, but looking back twenty years later, I understand that was a tall order for a boy of fourteen.

My knees ached all the way home. Mom's breathing was ragged. She rambled about what we'd have for dinner, how I needed to get homework done, how I should bathe Emma after I completed my assignments. But nothing made sense. Her thoughts toppled together like mudslides in a flood.

At the front door, she paused with her hand on the knob. I stood behind her, rooted to the bottom step. After a few moments, she handed Emma to me and said, "Jared, take your sister out to the back yard."

I nodded. "Sure, Mom. Come get me as soon as—"

"I will," she said, and opened the door onto a dark room. She called out in a quivering voice, "Milt?" Then louder and more forceful as she closed the door behind her: "Milt? Honey?" The sound of her shoes slapping the wood floor receded quickly.

In the back yard I got in the sandbox with Emma. With her yellow plastic spade she dug in the sand, poured it over her legs, her arms, dumped a scoop in her hair. I pulled the spade out of her hand and said, "No, Emma." Normally she cried when I took toys from her, but that day she crawled into my lap and nestled her back against my chest. I dug my comb out of my back pocket and worked it through her hair to get the sand out. A few minutes later she was asleep.

I couldn't wait any longer, couldn't leave Mom alone to clean up the mess. My brain felt detached from the rest of me. What I mean is, my thoughts were clear but I was numb, dazed as if I'd had the breath knocked out of me as I went through the list of things I'd need to do inside: put Emma in her room and close the door; wipe up the attic floor; help Mom get down the rickety steps; call whoever needed to be called. I carried Emma through the screen porch that led to the kitchen. Through a slit between the curtain and the window pane of the door, I saw Mom seated in Dad's chair at the table. She was smiling. I opened the door. She swiveled toward me, drew her hands to her face, and said, "Oh, Jared, I'm so sorry. I forgot to come get you."

"Where's Dad?"

She pointed to the far end of the table. I entered the room and there was Dad in Mom's chair, a stack of photo albums beside him. One of them lay open before him. His glasses teetered on the end of his bulbous nose

as he moved his finger across the page and downward.

I felt equally strong urges to hug him and to yell at him. Didn't he have any idea what he'd just put us through? *What about the pistol, Dad? Where'd you put it? What is it with these albums? You'd better have a sound reason for this behavior.*

They were his words, words he'd put to me many times. Not about the pistol, which he'd never allowed me to hold, but about any aberrant behavior. Of course, I couldn't talk to my father like that. I'm thirty-four years old now, and still can't imagine doing so.

Dad pressed his finger on the page and looked up. "Jared, come here, son. I want you to see something."

Emma stirred when I handed her to Mom, then nestled her head between Mom's neck and shoulder. I stood beside Dad and looked at a photograph I'd never seen before. "Who's that?" I said, pointing at a boy with a haircut that looked like someone had placed a bowl on his head and run a pair of shears around the edge. "Not the best-looking guy in the world, I'd say."

"What are you talking about, snaggletooth? That handsome devil is your father."

"No way."

"And these are your aunts and your grandmother."

I leaned over Dad's shoulder and studied the picture. He told me he'd turned ten years old a few days before the photograph was taken. The baby, Chloe, was almost two, and my other aunts, Meredith and Beatrice, were five and eight. Bonnets that looked like risen dough sat atop their heads. Dad's mother, who died before I was a year old, bore a vague resemblance to pictures I'd seen of her in her later years. I had to look for it, envision the many pictures I'd seen of a wizened woman, and then imagine a face without wrinkles and whiskers sprouting from her upper lip and chin.

"You have any more like this?" I asked.

He nodded toward the stack of albums.

I might have asked why he'd never pulled the albums out, but I knew the answer: Dad was not one for reminiscing. He didn't have a penchant for nostalgia. He scoffed at old men who talked about the good old days. "Yeah?" he said to one of Mom's uncles at a family reunion. "What was good about them? Let me take out your central heat and air, and let's see how those good old days feel." They didn't talk to each other the rest of the day.

Dad tapped his finger on the photograph. "It's time you know your people, Jared. You need to know where we've come from."

That evening after she put Emma to bed, Mom and I sat on either side of Dad on the den couch and studied the photographs as he flipped through them. Occasionally he paused to tell a story about one and another. I kept thinking how strange it was that Dad wasn't more upset about losing his job, how he had to be putting up a front, that sooner or later he'd break. Some of my friends' parents had lost jobs in the past few months. Several families lost their homes and had to leave the community. Danny Rikard's father, out of work for nine months, killed himself.

But that night, Dad seemed okay. We looked at pictures for almost two hours. Finally, as he closed an album, I said, "Dad, why aren't there any pictures of your father? How old was he when he died?"

I knew that my grandfather worked in a mill all his life because sometimes I asked Dad about him. He wouldn't say much, though. I wondered whether my grandfather was a bad man. Did he drink? Did he beat his wife and children? Did he chase women? I wasn't bold enough to ask such questions, but I couldn't help wondering, particularly because Dad was so reticent about him. One time I mustered the courage to say, "Did you and your dad get along, you know, like we do?"

Dad nodded and swiped his hand across his mouth. After that, I didn't ask any more questions.

That night, however, it felt right to ask. Maybe it was because I felt especially close to Dad, almost protective of him since he'd lost his job. Or maybe I sensed that he wanted me to ask. He'd said it was time for me to know my people.

Dad looked at the blue flame sparking around the biggest log on the fire. Mom put a hand on his leg, palm up, and he entwined his fingers with hers. She pursed her lips, looked him in the eye, and nodded.

Several times Dad started to speak but faltered. He shook his head and closed his mouth. It was like he was looking for a sure way in, a path he could follow without fear of getting lost. Finally he said, "He was young, Jared. Too young. Thirty-two when he died."

"How?"

Dad stumbled as if he'd taken the wrong path and found his way blocked. I'm sure he and Mom had talked about his father, but a man's talking to his wife and talking to his son require different forms of address. I couldn't have said as much then—I didn't have the language to articulate such an understanding—but I knew it, in the way that every child knows that his parents communicate with each other in ways that only they understand. A kind of secret code, I suppose, necessary to the vitality of the marriage.

My parents' code was at work that night. The way they transmitted understanding through the touch of their hands. The messages they sent each other with glances, shoulder nudges, a grunt, a clearing of the throat. Dad would not have gotten through the story without her help.

I understood that night, for the first time, how much my father loved his father. And how much he felt cheated by his death. Not cheated by his father himself, but by the world his father inhabited.

They were mill people, my grandparents. Papa—as I began to call him that night—went to work in the mill when he was thirteen. He had an eighth-grade education. Didn't mean he wasn't smart, Dad said; most men back then didn't advance past the eighth grade.

He was good with tools. An expert, Dad said. His eyes watered and he laughed as he recalled numerous times people would come to Papa asking for help with repair work. It didn't matter what needed repairing, they'd come with broken chairs, plows, small appliances. Papa had magic in his hands, Dad said. Mill people always told Dad that when Papa had a tool in his hand, it was impossible to tell where his hand ended and the tool began; each seemed a natural extension of the other.

I wanted to stay up all night listening to stories of my grandfather, of my father as a child, of their relationship. I tried to place myself in the stories, imagining myself first as Dad, then as Papa, then as a bystander observing the two of them.

That he was good with tools made the cause of his death all the more strange. This part of the story was tough for Dad. He got angry telling it, as if the wound from so many years ago had opened again and this time the cut wasn't clean and the blood was discolored by infection. The longer he spoke, the more intensely he stared at his right hand as though the wound were there, and the wider it opened, the deeper his anger went. Not rage. Anger that seeps deep into the heart and leaves you sick with the realization that what you're facing is far more powerful than you, that no matter where you turn, no one is there to help.

Dad said he and his mother and sisters were at the breakfast table early one morning when they heard footfall on the porch. Aunt Meredith slid out of her chair and scurried to the door. She always wanted to be the first one to greet Papa. She opened the door and stepped back when she didn't recognize the man who towered over her. "I knew him, though," Dad said. "Every boy in the mill village knew him. We hated him, too. Feared that one day we'd be working for him."

Dad said no one in the village liked the supervisor. He held his position over the workers as though he were a king and they were serfs not worthy of his respect.

That morning, however, the supervisor didn't look so high and mighty. He stood there on my grandparents' porch rolling his hat around in his hands and looking like a chicken bone was stuck in his throat. He stammered about how Pa was a good worker and no one knew exactly how it happened and it wasn't his—the supervisor's—fault, he'd just told Pa to fix the machine so that production wouldn't suffer on his shift. "Of course,

I knew," Dad said, "that he'd done more than tell Papa to fix it. He threatened him with the loss of his job. It's what he did every time something went wrong: a spindle broke, a carding machine didn't work properly, any piece of machinery malfunctioned, and Mr. Davis railed at the workers, all but accusing them of sabotaging the equipment."

Still the man blathered, not saying anything my grandmother could make sense of, until finally she said, "Speak up, man. What is it you're trying to tell me? Is Virgil hurt?"

Dad said the moment his mother asked the question, he knew the answer. "She probably knew it, too," he said, "but sometimes the mind can't accept what it already knows, if that makes any sense."

"It does," I said, and thought about the number of times over the past several months I hadn't been able to accept the fact that friends were being forced out of their homes, that their parents were being laid off, that they had to move in search of other opportunities. Not that I was denying the horrible truth of what was happening in our community; it just made no sense that something like that *could* happen. Who would evict my friends from their homes? Perhaps I feared we also might be evicted, that Dad wouldn't find another job, that we would have nowhere to go. I hadn't forgotten the pistol in the attic, either, or Danny Rikard's father.

Dad said what saved the supervisor from having to answer my grandmother's question was the arrival of the mill owner. His driver pulled up close to the porch and before he could park the car and get out and open the rear door for his boss, the man was out. He was dressed to kill, Dad said: three-piece suit, crisp shirt, tie, leather shoes. It was the first and, except for Papa's funeral, last time Dad ever saw him.

I suppose I learned more about my father that night than I'd ever known. Or maybe the disparate pieces of his life began to come together in a way I'd never seen them assembled before. I looked again at the picture of my grandmother and aunts and Dad, a boy with a bad haircut, an angry smirk, looking out onto a world he doesn't trust.

He didn't go into the gory details of Papa's death. But even the little that he did tell gave me enough to conjure a nightmarish sight: the sawmill blade clamping down on Papa's hand and chomping like a rabid dog, working its way up to the arm, the shoulder, finally taking the whole body. The reality would have been faster than that, of course: more like the body being sucked into a dark vortex. The nightmare seems worse because the crushing and devouring take so long, but I'm sure if I'd been there to see what actually happened, no nightmare would have matched the horror.

I hugged Dad fiercely that night before going to bed. When I pulled away, his shirt was wet where my face had been. In my room I lay awake thinking about the reason Dad gave for showing me the pictures: "It's time you know your people. You need to know where we've come from."

The longer I thought about it, the more desperate I became to distinguish between my people and where we'd come from. The difference seemed vital. I did want to know my people: the grandfather I'd never seen and the grandmother I had but couldn't remember. But I did not want to think about where they'd come from. Where we'd come from. All I could imagine when I thought about that was that mill where Papa died. I thought also of his old Army pistol in our attic, and of how weird it was that he'd survived the war only to be killed by his work, and of how Danny's father killed himself because he *didn't* have work. But the main thought I could not dispel even for a moment was of that sawmill blade. I fought sleep as long as I could, saying repeatedly to myself, "Don't dream about the blade. Don't dream about the blade." And I didn't.

But I did dream. I saw bodies. And faces. Lots of them, all fixed with horrid, lifeless expressions: mouths clamped shut, eyes so blank they seemed incapable of vision, necks elongated as if they'd been stretched by a hangman's noose. I knew, though I'd never seen it because it was torn down before I was born, that I was in my grandparents' old house watching my father and grandmother and aunts as they looked into the lifeless faces of the supervisor and the owner. And then many others appeared, making their way toward the rickety porch, all of them, like the owner, wearing dark suits, crisp shirts, ties, leather shoes. All of them, as Dad had said, dressed to kill.

DARIEN CAVANAUGH

Bateaus at dock, Edisto Park. Beulah Glover Photograph Collection, Accession no. 12239.31, Folder 3.
Courtesy of South Caroliniana Library, University of South Carolina, Columbia, S.C.

A Brief History of Navigation

At dawn the boats
rest in gentle currents
of low tide, tethered,
hull to port, to an old dock
while the land holds
the water of the small inlet
before opening up to the sea,
where the first boats learned
what rivers feed
as new sails carried them
south and oars pushed them north,
where white-bearded gods threw
gales and tons of brick
on soldier-sailors held
captive by goddess lovers
and Actium felt the last sigh
of 200 warships giving birth
to "peace" for 400 years,
where Spanish galleons wandered
waterways so long

their captains fell
in love with Gulf Coast manatees
before mermaids became myths,
where countless slimy things still
crawl and a single bird decides
the fate of great ships full of souls,
where monuments of self-
magnificence got caught
in the sensual music of neglect,
met the strength of water
holding itself, staying its course,
where rogue waves swallow
mountains of steel moving
Dutch tulips and Cambodian sex
slaves from shores that forgot their beauty,
and where brine wears away at hulls,
day by day,
until everything breaks and slips
into starless darkness.

LAUREL BLOSSOM

Greenville County Rt. 25. Marsh Photograph Collection, Folder 9883 180–198, Accession number 9883–183.

Courtesy of South Caroliniana Library, University of South Carolina, Columbia, S.C.

North

Most of the route is four-lane through Georgia.
If you leave by new moonlight, walking
Northwest to Jessup, then northeast to Ludowici.
If you follow the demons of your own hands.
If, as is said, the route, the road north crosses
Straight to the sign of the river, if you shun the
Second-run movie fun house, reeling, distorted
Mirror misty with the breath of the dead.

If alongside I-20 you flee, just outside town,
Footsteps beating faster past Edgefield, Greenwood,
Where the heart ghosts keep their abandoned home,
If you hear the song of their singing. If barefoot
You reach the far foothills, if you rest,
Little traveler, before you suffer
Your fear, your fate, to the next unwritten line.
You have come to the rising, blue martyrdoms

Of your longing. From the border, if you follow
Your feet, your freeway, if it sends you back
With relief to brown dirt, the flat rock

They told you to touch for good luck. Then again
North if through Arden (oh, ardent!), through Biltmore
Forest (oh, built more, less forest!) and Asheville,
City of bone, to fishless (ah, hunger!) Woodfin, to
    Weaverville
Weaveless (oh, raiment! oh, rags!), northwesterly if
    you take
Your hard way through Marshall and Hot Springs,
Hope rising, (thou rascal, oh, Roosevelt!) (thou blessed!)
Into the wilds of tent-tent (oh, shelterless!) Tennessee.

Twenty miles to old Newport, if, as before,
You choose if to go: west, first
To Knoxville, where up, how down, or east
Through the Cumberland Gap, its tunnel, emerging,
Like spring from (Persephone, ah!) underground.
Dangerous, rain-soaked, sun-burned, alone,
But close now, roads converging at Corbin, connecting
Through London, Berea, Richmond, Lexington,
Dry Ridge, to Covington at the (oh my oh!) Ohio River,
The (ah, most Jordan!) State line. Run, Eliza, run!

Family. Armstrong Family Papers, 1900–1930. Courtesy of South

Caroliniana Library, University of South Carolina, Columbia, S.C.

11 *Tanka for the Neighbors*

/1/
It's there in the in-
between: the facility between
laughter or . . . not-laughter;
there, between the crooks of her slender shoulders

between the hinges on her thin corner-smiles; inter-
stices when she dresses for summer while
most of us dawdle in spring.

/2/
He sometimes takes their dreams and indexes them
on bar napkins: sketches of ariettas, per-chance operettas up-lilting

off into the duskiest dusk when sun kills moon—little vignettes of lust:
walking the roadbed in silver-screened fields, stealing kisses,

lit cigarettes in the doorway, two bodies stretching themselves over Lake Michigan
like a wake—a cacophony in C:

their song is a front-facing brokenness, at times; at times:
a bloodline that syncopates when he soft-slips his bare palm into hers.

/3/
On Wednesday's she eats
in the park, meek and girdled:
looking birds, wings crooked,
covering their waddle-walks.
They want her to take them back:

into the sallow, into dark and into the haimish.
They call to her, *come back,*
but the pedagogy of her flesh is un-

breakable carri-
on: unflappable: what's hers
is hers to carry
on: when all those apertures—
when all those fissures—are gone.

/4/
It's in the way she reads the little notes
he leaves—one leg tucked the other, cradled
on the couch: slip a hand between knock-knees or

tell him you love him,
whichever is easiest.
He carries you on him:
vestigial and staccato,
in the in-between.

JULIA ELLIOTT

Miscellaneous—Residence—Interior—parlor. George LaGrange Cook Photograph Collection, Box 5; Temporary num. 137. Courtesy of South Caroliniana Library, University of South Carolina, Columbia, S.C.

August 1886

Uncorseted, unbathed, jittery from a second cup of coffee, you loll on the second-story balcony with your book (a leather-bound edition of *Middlemarch,* its spine velvety with green mold), watching for storms. Your mother has been fighting the mold all summer, snatching brocade drapery from rods, marching down to the garden with her battle face on, a phalanx of black maids behind her. She hangs the heavy fabric in the sun, beats the filth out of it, for too much washing will spoil the nap. In this weather, nothing quite dries anyway. Your nightgown is damp. Your dark, lanky hair is damp. Your *soul is cloaked in damp fog,* or so you have scratched in your diary with your father's fancy fountain pen.

Your father, once a sprightly surgeon for the Confederate medical corps (he still brags about the day he performed fifty-two amputations with a bone saw), is now a waddling walrus of a man, all woolen waistcoats and waxed moustaches, indigestion and bookish opinions. Of course he has opinions about you. A year at Vassar has transformed you. You left last August, a chattering, plump-cheeked chatterbox, returning in May as a pallid *neurasthenic.* Two much intellectual stimulation has thrown your menstrual cycle out of whack, he opines. Your organs of generation, starved of vital energy, are,

shriveling he opines. Between bites of liver pudding, terminology sputters from his lips: *uterine atrophy* (belch), *sterility* (belch), *race suicide* (belch).

You hear him now, puttering around in the library below, removing dangerous books from the shelves—*Das Kapital, Also sprach Zarathustra, The Pearl: A Magazine of Facetiae and Voluptuous Reading.* You hear your mother on the side lawn, beating a carpet with a broom. You stand. You peer over the railing. There she is: a robust woman of forty-five, cursed with superfluous energies (even though she has borne four children), thrashing the living hell out of a rug. The maids watch. When they try to give Miss Lily a break, she snarls. The maids are there for moral support, especially now that it has started to drizzle again. Your mother shrieks, waves her arms at the maids. They hustle to pull the heavy rug from the clothesline, haul it onto the side porch.

You turn back to storm-watching. Now you see it: a gray hullabaloo floating above the horizon. It flies toward you, throwing off pale yellow jags of lightening. A gust of damp coolness lifts your limp hair. Your gown balloons. The air glows, the sickly gold of sulfur. You recall the stomach-churning feeling of flight in dreams—the panicky wonder as you float over a lawn at night, rising higher into the air until you are whisked up into star-speckled darkness by a power you did not know you possessed.

———⟞⟝———

When he sees you reading *On Woman's Right to Suffrage* at supper, your father threatens to cover you in leeches. He is joking, of course. He is not a monster, and his mustaches twitch as he smirks. You sit in the moldy dining room over a bowl of oyster stew, rain falling in the gray twilight, as your father lectures your mother on the properties of mold.

"The spores are always there," he says, "lurking. But now the atrociously humid weather conditions enable the species to thrive."

"Natural selection?" asks your mother.

"Not exactly," your father says.

Just this morning, you opened a drawer and gasped with perverse pleasure when you saw a velvety jungle of mold growing on your black stockings. A miniature enchanted forest, a delicate shade of greenish-blue. You haven't worn stockings since May.

"Tomorrow," says your mother. "I'm going to drown the entire infernal house with vinegar. Every last crystal on every chandelier will be scrubbed. Every handkerchief laundered. This is war. And I will prevail."

Your mother lived through the actual war, of course, barricaded in a malarial Sumter plantation with three children for the worst of it. And her gray eyes spark with fury. She turns these eyes upon you.

"Percival Tewksbury is back from France," she says.

The oyster in your mouth tastes metallic, as though boiled with nickels, and you are suddenly aware that you hold a small exotic animal upon the pink cushion of your tongue. You chew the animal to mush. You swallow.

"I hope he is well," you say, turning back to your book. You do not say, "Percival Tewksbury is a goat in a waistcoat." You do not say, "I'll bet he caught the pox from some trollop." You lift a silver spoon to your lips and take a slurp of fishy milk.

"Marriage would cure her megrims," your father jokes. But then, he's not really joking, is he? And the whole issue is, of course, a cliché. How many novels have you read that are devoted precisely to this dilemma? The spirited young heroine harassed by two specters: gaunt, yellow spinsterhood hunched on one shoulder; fat, pink marriage leering on the other. Though you would like to have a child one day, you can't imagine dealing with a baby right this minute. Your two older sisters have already spawned litters, while your dipsomaniacal brother fails to distinguish himself in medical school.

"I think I'll call upon my dear friend Eloise today," you say, and your parents exchange dark looks.

——————

Eloise, a widow with no children, taps a few drops of Mrs. Winslow's Soothing Syrup into her coffee. Lounging on the east veranda in the shadow of her stone mansion (in which the ghost of her dead husband fusses with his hoary whiskers in eternal agitation), Eloise stretches. She spreads the wings of her lilac kimono to greet you. You glance up at the turret in which a maiden aunt is stashed (Aunt Giblet, poor relation and befuddled chaperone, is, of course, embroidering some scrap of muslin).

"Look." Eloise flutters her wings. "The sun."

"Not for long." You point. "Look at those clouds."

Thick, curdy, they fester over the sea. A mixed-race maid no older than fourteen brings coffee and biscuits. Two houseguests drift out: a poet with glowing eyes and a receding chin (Everett Owling, Eliose's second cousin, whose father died in the war), and an intense female landscape painter, her strangely tiny head overpowered by a tempest of Pre-Raphaelite curls (Adelaide Tisk, Eloise's late husband's "difficult" niece). When Eloise brags about your year at college, you do not mention your current dilemma (wishy-washy parents, strained finances). Instead, you jump right into the brisk, choppy river of banter and speculation, holding your own on such subjects as the Woman Question, the Indian Question, the cranial structures of the various races of men, *The Origin of Species,* the Übermensch, Goethe's *Theory of Colours,* James's *Portrait of a Lady,* negative capability, free love, the naturist movement, Theosophy, physiognomy, animal magnetism, Zulus, photography, motorcars, electricity, the Sublime, Socialism, and the scandalous adulterous liaisons of Patricia P. Pinkney, whose husband resembles a bald possum.

Everett Owling declares that he is an anarchist. Adelaide Tisk sets up her easel. Eloise pulls out her bottle of Mrs. Winslow's Soothing Syrup and fortifies her third cup of coffee with a generous splash. Aunt Giblet emerges, wipes her dewy brow with a handkerchief, and sits in a wrought-iron garden chair. As Everett Owling recites a poem called "The Noble Negress," he pauses between stanzas to stare soulfully at Eloise's pretty young housemaid. Thunder grumbles. The air turns gold.

"I swanny," opines Aunt Giblet. "I do believe it will rain again."

"Really?" says Eloise, with a hint of restless cruelty. "You don't say?"

Aunt Giblet stands up. Her phantom bustle pops out with a rusty squeak. She sits down again, and the contraption collapses.

"Yes," she says, taking up her embroidery, "it will indeed."

"Bless your heart." Eloise chuckles. The young widow stands, paces, gazes out at the sea. Once again, you are struck with the thought that Eloise has no idea what to do with herself. You fight back a surge of bile. If you had a mansion and a fortune, a dead coot of a husband and distant parents, what would you do? You would have a camera. You would have a motorcar. You would grow Oriental poppies on the front lawn. You would have a darkroom, a laboratory, an aviary packed with exotic birds. You would rise at an industrious hour and write novels. You would fortify your musty library with the latest books. Deck out the west turret in walnut and plum velvet and make it your study. Open the windows. Let the clouds float right through the room.

"I hear there's an automagnatist at Wisteria Inn," Eloise says, turning from the sea.

"What, pray tell, is an automagnatist?" asks Aunt Giblet, rising, in alarm, with a fierce bustle squeak.

"Mesmerist, spiritualist, psychologist, quack," says Everett. "I've heard of him."

"We should go see him." Eloise plops back into her chaise.

You recall that last summer, just after her husband passed and Eloise was diagnosed with a mild case of hysteria, she'd gone to see a certain doctor in Radcliffeborough. After undergoing a forty-five-minute pelvic massage, Eloise experienced a hysterical paroxysm that offered temporary respite from her night terrors. The summer before that, Eloise was freshly married, initiated into the mysteries of love by forty-six-year-old Monroe Potter. The summer before that, you were both still students at Josephine Randolph Finishing School for Young Ladies, reading *Lady Bumtickler's Revels* (filched from your dissolute brother) and falling into endless laughing fits.

You still love Eloise; she's just a little silly, which is why her parents pushed her on Potter. But now she's as free as she could ever dream of being. Free and jumping out of her chair, circling Adelaide Tisk like a buzzard.

"Maybe I should try painting," Eloise says.

Adelaide grunts, keeping her small eyes fixed on the storm.

You admire her brushwork, the glowing gray of her floating cumuli. Somehow she has captured the sulfurous light, the feeling of pressure in the air just before a storm breaks.

As the squall sweeps over the sea, Everett Owling lectures you on the pathetic fallacy. His tone is condescending and flirtatious. His eyes are soft and lovely, his chin absurd. You imagine kissing him. You shudder with a strange mix of repulsion and desire as you feel the first drops hit your cheeks.

"It's raining; it's raining," Aunt Giblet cries, running for the portico, her bustle crooked.

Adelaide packs her paint set with fierce efficiency. Eloise reclines upon her chaise and opens her arms to the storm.

"Good girl," says Everett, squatting on the edge of Eloise's chair. "One should not cower from the rain. One should embrace the rain."

You jog toward the porch. And it feels good to run, despite the pinch of your corset. When you reach the house, you keep going, darting across the empty ballroom, trotting up the marble steps, up another flight to the third floor, skirting the nursery, the desolate maids' quarters, finally flying up a narrow staircase to the attic where you step out onto the roof. The sky is clear. There is a spell of soft, blue coolness to savor after the storm. But in five minutes you feel hot again. The monster sun is roaring, boiling the dew, filling the air with a zillion invisible droplets.

You are up in the throbbing night, moving through the house, all windows open wide. Crickets shriek in the darkness beyond the screens. In the kitchen you stumble upon your father, hunched in his nightshirt, tearing at a turkey leg with his small yellow teeth. He grins like a lycanthrope, smoothes his wild hair.

"Insomnia?" he asks.

"A touch," you say.

As you rifle for biscuits, you feel his clinical eyes upon you. You have lost a few pounds. Your complexion is sallow. Reproductive energies fester within you, ovaries chocked with dormant eggs, diverted potential that might implode, blooming into luxuriant hysteria. You read too much. Your small, delicate brain, which evolved to nest and nurture, seethes with deformed embryonic ideas. Your first week home from school, when he caught you with a copy of *Lucifer the Lightbearer,* he knew he had made a mistake. He confiscated the "trash," shaking his head as he read its mission aloud: "to help woman break the chains that for ages have bound her to the rack of man-made law, spiritual, economic, industrial, social and especially sexual." Red-faced (he could not look at you) he tossed the newspaper into the stove and stomped off to consult your mother.

"Hungry?" he asks you now.

"Starved," you say, discovering, at last, the tin of cinnamon biscuits that Vic, the cook, made that morning.

You have not yet discussed the fall term, even though school is scheduled to begin in two weeks. You are enrolled, but there is the issue of funds. There is the issue of what your father calls a *touch of neurasthenia.* There is the issue of your recent birthday (twenty) and your failure to pursue a marriage befitting your age, station, and social graces (you can play the piano with romantic flair, discuss poetry, elegantly wield a pickle fork). There is the issue of your cavorting with a crowd of untethered youths (poor Eloise and her parasites). And you can't help smirking as you consider your father's imagination in full riot. On the one hand, the poor man fears that you are a sex- (and baby-) starved hysteric. On the other, he fears that you are indulging in opium-fuelled orgies with syphilitic poets.

When you were little, he read you *Alice's Adventures in Wonderland* and Grimm's *Children's and Household Tales,* laughing at the dark flourishes—quirky amputations, magical comas, blood-stained keys. He taught you how to chloroform butterflies and dissect earthworms and control a spirited horse. He personally directed your studies in biology and mathematics. But now he stands in the lamplight, barefooted, night-shirted, mustaches drooping, eyes flickering with fear. He thinks he's made a monster of you. You have a sudden urge to fall into his arms and breathe in the naïve and reassuring scent of his mustache wax—an urge you have not felt for years. Instead you smile and brush past him. You hurry back to your room, back to your insomnia, back to your ridiculous, albeit forbidden, book (*Autobiography of a Flea*).

Mildred Mood's garden party is sparsely attended. Thick, curdy clouds convolute over the city. Your skirts are damp from the drizzly carriage ride. And your mother is ticked, not only because you refused to wear a bustle, but also because you referred to the contraption as "prosthetic buttocks," sneering at her beribboned and festooned artificial posterior as she struggled to achieve comfortable seating in the carriage. At least you're wearing a corset. At least you're sporting a silk gown with a trim waist that highlights your "reproductive assets."

"Please don't talk that way at the party," your mother advised.

Now that you are finally here, she droops with disappointment. After surveying the miserable company (mostly mothers with dull girls in their mid-twenties; a sprinkling of homely, fortyish bachelors), a look of defeat washes over your mother's face (the same look you saw just yesterday when she discovered yet another linen closet colonized by mold). When she sighs and joins a trio of gossipy matrons on the porch, you feel a sick stab of guilt. You accept a glass of peach punch from a maid. You consume a cucumber sandwich. You watch the clouds, hoping for a storm—anything to shake up this farce of upper-middle-class aspiration.

When you spot Percival Tewksbury making his grand entrance, you hide behind a cluster of blue delphiniums.

Twenty-nine years old, squeezed into a waistcoat of canary yellow satin, his fleshy pink face gleaming like a broiled ham, he approaches various belles seated on the clusters of damp garden furniture. His dissolute lips twist into a wry, condescending grin. He's used to a flashier crowd, of course, though his mother is Mildred's cousin, so here he is with his sparkling watch chain and calfskin boots.

When he sees you, he laughs. He seizes a glass of punch from an unattended tray and strolls over.

"Well, well, well," he says. "The college girl returns."

"Actually, I've been trapped in this putrid town for three months," you say.

"Putrid," he says. "That's funny. Don't tell me you've become a poetess."

"Novels are more my thing." (You vow to start your novel the very next day.)

"Is your head reeling from the sparkling *bon mots* on display at Cousin Mildred's delightful soiree?"

"I just had a conversation about Dostoyevskian mysticism with Cecelia Tuten." You glance at poor Cecelia, who's feeding her terrier a fritter.

"She's quite the bluestocking." Percival titters and then whips a brass flask from a secret waistcoat pocket.

"Fancy a drop?" He enhances his punch with a generous douse.

"What's the elixir?"

"Bourbon."

"That will do."

You hold out your cup, thinking he might be poisoning you with laudanum or some more exotic substance acquired on his recent travels, during which he is reputed to have gone whoring with a Russian count.

You get tipsy. The sun pops out. The pulsing of cicadas intensifies, as though the whole summer day is vibrating. Like all women of your class, you are burning up, of course, insanely overdressed for the weather. And Percival Tewksbury's enflamed lips keep brushing your left ear as he whispers his witticisms.

"Now there's an interesting maiden." He nods toward Patricia Radcliff, who's just emerged onto the back porch. "A cross between the Mona Lisa and a praying mantis. She has that cryptic smile, that swiveling, triangular, cannibalistic head."

You have to admit that Percival can be clever, but mostly at the expense of others. You have to admit that he exudes a certain animal magnetism, that the feel of his breath on your ear lobe creates a tingling sensation in your nether zone. But *what,* you want to ask him, is he *doing* with his *energies* since he dropped out of school? He travels. He knows his way around the restaurants and saloons and brothels of major European cities, but to what purpose? You envy his freedom, of course, the ability to walk unmolested through a foreign city, alone, at night, reputation and body safe from assault. But you stuff your resentment into the back of your mind, for you are a little drunk. And the delphiniums are glowing. And it strikes you that the young women are arranged like flowers in a florist's shop, skirts expanded like hopeful petals. Ugly men hop among them like toads, sniffing, ogling for spots of blight.

You retreat into the gnarled darkness of a magnolia tree. And now Percival Tewksbury is kissing you. His hands are hot upon your bosom. You do not calculate the possibilities of a marriage proposal (you would never marry Percival Tewksbury, not if you were thirty and crippled and he was the last man on earth). You allow yourself to float into the experience. Reveling in the biology of kissing, you recall certain passages form *Autobiography of a Flea*. You slip your hand under Percival's waistcoat, palpate the silk of his shirt, the warm pudge of his belly. Of course, your mother is calling you now, her voice hopeful, yet shrill. You assume she saw you slip into the shadows with Percival. You assume she's been sitting on pins and needles, hoping to give the young man enough time to *declare his feelings,* but not enough to *take advantage* of you.

His waistcoat, you notice, is embroidered with violet birds. A constellation of tiny scabs surrounds his lush mouth (shaving cuts). He smells of sweat and bourbon and some loud Eau de Cologne. And he is moving away from you, back into the company. You emerge from the shade. Your mother spots you, relaxes, lowers herself back into her wicker chair.

You wake up. The hag is crouching on your chest. Your mother, from the low country, has always described the condition this way, while your father, a man of science, prefers the term *sleep paralysis.* Vic, the cook, is also plagued by the hag. On certain mornings, looking puny, she'll inform you that the hag *rode* her all night, a prospect that has terrified you for as long as you can remember. Despite your lifelong fear of this demon, the hag has never visited you. Now, in the muggy thick of night, she squats on your chest. Though you feel her weight, you can't see her. You imagine that she's naked, or clothed in a rank swaddling of rags. You think you feel a pair of withered buttocks pressing against your sternum. You think

you smell the oniony stench of feet, fungus-blasted toenails, putrid breath wheezing from a toothless mouth.

The hag hails from swamps and marshes. She thrives in malarial air. Travels in fog banks, floats up from outhouses and oozes through windows.

You think you hear her snorting. You think you hear her cackling. Or is that the crickets screaming? Summer is almost over, and the crickets are in a panic to mate and die.

You try to move your arms. You try to move your legs. Even your lips are paralyzed, your tongue as dead as a lump of pickled beef. Only your eyeballs move, rotating in your skull as you scrutinize the uncanny darkness of your childhood bedroom.

"Perhaps next year we will have the funds," your father says. And then he picks up his silver spoon.

On this date last year you were in a passenger car, flying up the coast with your heart in your throat. Today, you eat with your father in the dim dining room, the world outside a haze of drizzle. You stare down at the boiled creatures on your plate, pink crustaceans curled like fetuses. Your mother is abed, exhausted from battle. She has lost the war with mold. The brocade drapes are green with rioting fungi. Black mildew speckles the walls. Fuzzy organisms creep up the chair legs. You imagine that you are trapped in a fairy tale curse—a hundred years of rain, perpetual twilight, a princess moving in a somnambulistic daze through a house velvety with emerald mold. You imagine a series of princes—Percival Tewksbury, Everett Owling, Christian Capers Venning—each more ridiculous than the last. You sigh. You pick a sand vein from a shrimp, the digestive tract, a murky strand of shit.

Your father does not make eye contact with you. Grumbling over his newspaper, he absently receives the ministrations of Vic the cook as though she is some disembodied spirit appointed by heaven to attend him. He holds up a filthy plate, and it vanishes. He spills water on the table, and a rag materializes to sop it up. He belches, pushes his plate away, and two seconds later, a tumbler of whiskey fortified with Browns Iron and Quinine Bitters appears before him. What would happen if Vic disappeared, you wonder, and he was surrounded by floating napkins, levitating cutlery, placemats flying through the air like magic carpets? Would he even notice?

⚬⚬⚬

"I don't know what's worse, the heat or the rain." Eloise flings her restless body around the east veranda. She's on her second glass of iced tea, her bottle of Mrs. Winslow's Soothing Syrup open on a wicker side table. The bamboo shades are open, but there is no breeze so speak of.

Everett Owling dozes on the chaise. Adelaide Fisk paints him with ferocious concentration. Eyes flickering up and down his body, she bites her bottom lip. Her dress is patched with sweat, her hair twisted atop her head, her nape dewy. When you see the square-jawed, glowing Adonis on her canvas, you understand that she and the poet are *having relations.* Of course they are! What else would explain their lingering in this infernal limbo? Lurid and absurd imagery fills your head (you have been reading Sir Richard Burton's translation of the *Kama Sutra,* filched from your father's secret stash of books,

despite the queasy feeling you get every time you stumble upon one of his prim annotations).

The two months of rain that recently plagued you now seem like part of the primordial past—wet, ferny, Paleozoic. There's not a speck of cloud in a sky. The ocean is like pounded pewter. The sun, naked and florid and fat, burns your eyes. Mid-morning, and you are already insufferably hot. You left the house uncorseted. Your stomach presses lewdly against the thin fabric of your dress.

"Where's Aunt Giblet?" you ask.

"In her turret." Eloise points at the ceiling. "Spasms, megrims, gripes."

"Bless her heart." You smile.

"I can't stand it anymore," says Eloise. "I'm going in."

You follow her into the dark house. Everett and Adelaide linger on the porch. Eloise drifts among velvet sofas, finally sits down. You join her. She seizes your hand. Her breath smells of vanilla and some darker chemical. Her pupils are dilated, her irises silver, her eye-whites shot with veins.

"Let's go on a trip," she says. "Let's go to Greece, Rome, Egypt, Turkey. Why not?"

"Impossible," you say, though you can't help envisioning the two of you in white linen frocks and sunhats, approaching the sphinx. You see its cryptic face, its cobra mantel, its crumbling, syphilitic nose.

"Why impossible?" Eloise says. "We could take Aunt Giblet."

You laugh. "Curiouser and curiouser."

"Just think about it," she says.

"Rest assured, I will think of little else for the next few days, and then be done with the fantasy."

"There's something else I want to tell you." Eloise

is whispering now, even though you are alone in a vast room. "I went to see the automagnatist."

"The what?"

"The mesmerist or whatever, the electrical psychologist, and he—*they*—are, well, I can't quite describe it. You have to experience it yourself."

Last summer, Eloise said the same thing about that lady's doctor in Radcliffeborough.

"He's at the Wisteria Inn, on the top floor, suite 333. The password is *mercury.*"

"Password? That's ridiculous."

"Trust me." She smirks, massages your sweaty palms with her thumbs. "Just try it."

Your mother is napping. Your father is at his office, fussing over the malfunctioning bodies of his rich elderly patients—disintegrating digestive systems, floundering hearts, organs shriveling or herniating or leaking. You scribble a note—*Gone to Eloise's for tea*—and get Robert, the gardener, to drive you downtown. You wonder, not for the first time, how much your parents pay him, and finding your next train of thought uncomfortable (how and where Robert might live on such a salary), you marvel at the dreamlike emptiness of the streets, the parched yellow trees and gray grass. Cicadas throb. This morning, you found one dead in the grass. You picked it up, held the stinking jewel in your palm, and decided to visit the automagnatist.

Robert drops you off on Princess Street, and now you are walking alone on Fulton, the afternoon sun in your face. Two black men walk by, hauling the trussed corpse of a hog. A painted woman in pink satin loiters under an arch of parched jasmine. She grins at you, revealing a missing front tooth. A glossy black carriage crawls to a stop. Its side door opens. An ancient hand emerges— pale, yellow-nailed, a chicken claw fringed with lace. The woman climbs in, her voluptuous bustle swaying. She is spirited off to some secret part of the city—an opium den, you fancy, for you have just finished *Confessions of an English Opium Eater,* and your imagination ferments with exotic squalor. You imagine half-naked yellow people in cryptic clouds of smoke, the occasional bearded bohemian lounging among them, musty embroidered curtains, sweaty pillows, candle-light, body odor, whispers.

You step onto the porch of the Wisteria Inn. The building is leprous with flaking paint, patches of stucco visible, gray as old bones. When you see no one at the front desk, you slip into a shabby parlor, also empty. You spot a staircase, rush up it in a flurry of rustling skirts. You cruise the second floor, its series of doors painted a sickly mustard. A door at the end of the hallway pops open, and an ancient man in a wheelchair springs out, a specter in a lace nightshirt. He squeaks toward you.

"I'm looking for the stairs," you say, noticing them, at last, in an alcove beyond him. You squeeze past the old man, who emits a goatish bleat, and rush up another flight.

At last you are standing in front of room 333, its door painted the deep fleshy brown of roasted liver. You knock. The door opens. You walk into a windowless receiving room. The dark wainscoting gleams with fresh lacquer. You struggle with dizziness (you have just trotted up two flights of stairs, your corset is laced too tight, and the spirituous smell of the lacquer goes right to your head). Behind a vast oak desk, a tiny man with pert mustaches sits, his spectacles twinkling in the half-light. You marvel at the glossiness of his pomaded hair. You note that he is absurdly handsome, dainty, dapper, shorter than you.

"Mercury," you whisper.

"Of course. Mrs. Potter has already settled your account."

"Account?" you murmur, but the secretary ignores your indiscretion.

When he comes closer, you see that his face is powdered, his cheeks caked with pink rouge. He opens a set of double doors, ushers you into a hot drawing room. Seats you upon the lumpy cushions of a brocade sofa and withdraws. You have the strange sensation that the couch is stuffed with dead minks. You can't imagine why, though you do detect a faint muskiness in the air, probably due to the number of human bodies that have sat sweating on this very sofa. You glance around: mahogany paneling, thickly swaddled windows, the glint of gilded picture frames. You squint at murky portraits, making out bits and pieces of people: the feral white eyebrows of an elderly patriarch, the ivory swell of a female bosom, the proud, constipated smirk of a red-robed judge. When a breeze whisks aside some window drapery, a circle of light floats across the far wall, illuminating a silver tea service. And then you hear the rich croak of the automagnatist.

"Shall we have some light?"

The globes of the chandelier above you swell with incandescence. You think of sea medusas, fireflies, the moons of Jupiter. You wonder if the man is a stage magician. Although you are aware of electricity, and you once witnessed the exhibition of a galvanoscope at Vassar, you can't imagine how this old inn could be rigged up with the necessary wires, conductors, generators.

The automagnatist steps into the light. Squat, hairless, moist and pallid, as though he belongs to the family *Amphibia* and has just slithered from a swamp, he stands in a tweedy waistcoat and trousers, perspiration upon his skin. In the stark illumination, you see instruments and small machines crammed together upon the marble-topped table behind him, objects that you assumed, in the half-dark, were clocks, sculptures, assorted knick-knackery. Of course, you take note of the curious chair standing right beside the instrument table. Upholstered in wine velvet, fitted out with wires that run from its padded head-rest to the compact, black motor stashed under its seat like an insect egg ready to drop, the whole contraption resting on a flared base that reminds you of metallic spider legs, the chair fills you with a blend of longing and dread. You want to flee from the chair and the clammy automagnatist. But you also want to sit in the chair and let the strange man strap you into it (there are black canvas straps with silver buckles affixed to the arms and foot-rest). And when the automagnatist summons you with a firm gaze and a flick of his wrist, you move toward the uncanny chair.

The automagnatist's assistant is the same as the secretary, you are almost positive, though now the delicate man is wearing a white lab coat, his mustaches have vanished, and you think you detect a hint of dried glue above his upper lip. As he buckles you into the chair, you are almost positive that *he* is a *she,* especially when you notice the telltale lumps of breasts that you suspect have been bound with bandage gauze, the kind your father used to wrap around the gangrenous legs of soldiers. You recall a girl from school who would sometimes crawl out of her dormitory window dressed in men's clothing. Once, out walking in the early morning, you saw her skulking through shrubs.

As the assistant retrieves a crystal beaker, an assortment of vials, and begins concocting, siphoning, decanting, you wonder if she is the automagnatist's wife. You imagine them entwined in one of the more acrobatic poses from the *Kama Sutra,* the lithe assistant coiled around the toad-shaped automagnatist and writhing like a snake. With a smirk, as though reading your filthy thoughts, the assistant offers you a tumbler of glowing yellow liquid. You recall your brother as a six-year-old boy, slaughtering fireflies one hot summer night, smearing his naked chest with bioluminescent gore as your father lectured him on the properties of *luciferins.*

You take the shining drink. It burns going down, drawing attention to your esophagus, reminding you of your inner *arcana,* the labyrinths of intestines twisting within you, pumping organs and glands, thousands of dainty valves fluttering to direct the flow of blood, hormones, electricity.

The automagnatist's pale, bald head floats beneath the orbs of the electric chandelier. He takes your temperature. Palpates your pulse points. Presses a silver stethoscope into your cleavage. The automagnatist plucks a curious device from his instrument tray—a flexible, segmented metallic object that resembles an insect abdomen covered in wispy filaments. When he slides the contraption down your left arm, the fibers catch upon your hairs, leaving an electrical tingling sensation. When

he slides it along your throat, the device hums. The automagnatist grunts. His assistant slips a satin blindfold over your eyes.

"Be very still," she whispers. "Please allow me to remove your stockings to access your feet. Otherwise, you shall remain clothed."

You nod. You feel prickles upon your inner wrists. Prickles upon your throat, behind your ears. At the top of your cranium.

Someone is removing your shoes. Adjusting your skirts, pushing up the legs of your pantaloons. Someone us unfastening your garters. Peeling down your stockings. You feel the same electrical prickles behind your knees, upon your ankles, between your toes.

"You are floating in thick, warm liquid," says the automagnatist.

You imagine a puddle of brown, primeval mud, slithering with green salamanders. You feel yourself floating.

"You are getting younger and younger," says the automagnatist. "You are a lass. You are a child. You are a toddler. Your body is shrinking, growing tinier and softer until you are an infant. You cannot walk. You cannot talk. You are small and fat, naked and damp, sliding toward black nothingness."

At first you are acutely aware of the automagnatist's voice, the croaky tenor, crackling with excess mucus, the British accent that you suspect is fake, the amateurish poetic devices. But then you lose track of the automagnatist's words. Submerged in images, you succumb to the flow of sensations.

You hover over a bed, a buoyant blob of pure spirit, gazing down at your parents, two keen young bodies coiled together to form a grunting, two-backed beast.

Before you can process the obscenity (the grimacing faces, the sweaty nudity, the thick, animal panting) the vision multiplies as you witness the two couplings that created each of your parents, and then the four couplings that created your parents' parents, and then the eight couplings that created your parents' parents' parents, and so on, each coupling sprouting another pair of couplings, until you are surrounded by a swarm of copulators, buzzing in the air like mosquitoes, pumping, pulsing, glowing.

You take a moment to spy on a particularly vigorous set of great, great, great, grandparents, procreating on a hemp mattress. Another duo of ancestors fucks languidly upon a pile of straw, the woman perched atop the man. Another is screwing in the grass, the male mounting the female from behind, and you notice the hairiness of their limbs, the massiveness of their jaws, the thick, leathery ridges on their brows. The ape-people growl. The sky shimmers with primordial stars.

You enter the body of your hominid ancestor, the female, of course, just as she wakes up. You lie in the grass, listening to insects and morning birds. The rising sun looks the same as it has always looked, though you are too distracted to pay much attention to it, because something is rustling through the bushes behind you. You sniff. Upon smelling the rank, yellow musk of a leopard, you leap to your feet and dash across the savannah. You scramble up a tree. The leopard, spotting a stray Dik-dik fawn, abandons you. You leap from the tree. You bend toward a puddle to drink. As another male hominid slinks up behind you, you float up above your body. You flit around in the air, relieved to have escaped the

fluttery, fearful, odor-crammed consciousness of your ape ancestor.

Before you can enjoy the delicious weightlessness, however, you are stuffed into the body of a wild sow, just as she is taken by a boar. Next you enter the crouched form of a spotted hyena, grinning and panting as a male mounts her. You become an elephant cow, a tiny terrestrial bear, and then an enormous prehistoric rat. You become a stork, a newt, a perch, a leech. And then you are a termite queen, fat with a thousand ovaries, spewing a multitude of eggs. You are a clam, releasing twenty million gametes into warm murk. At last, you are an amoeba, complete unto yourself, blissfully budding, splitting, multiplying. You are a microscopic galaxy, each atom a solar system whirring inside of you. You are a universe.

"You are vast, nebulous, birthing moons and stars," says the automagnatist, who has been speaking to you all this time, you realize, in his mesmerizing, croaky voice. It takes a moment to remember who you are; where you are. You blush. You can't see. You pat your arms and legs to make sure that you are clothed. Yes, you are, though you have sweated through your shift, and your dress is damp. You are still wearing undergarments. Much to your relief, you are not covered in musky fur, nor equipped with clammy gills. The automagnatist's assistant is removing your blindfold, nodding discreetly, helping you out of the curious chair.

The automagnatist's assistant, once again mustachioed, once again distinctly male, accompanies you downstairs. He nods, releases you as though you are a cat, and locks the door behind you.

"Curiouser and curiouser."

You keep whispering this childhood incantation to calm yourself, for many hours have passed, and you are walking through a dark city alone. A headache makes it difficult to think. A chalky bitter film coats your tongue. Of course, Robert is not idling on Jasmine Street as he was supposed to be. Of course, he has long since rushed in a panic to your parents and confessed that he dropped their defenseless daughter off on Princess—*Heaven knows why.* You imagine your mother, pacing, collapsing into chairs only to fly out of them and proclaim, with a shake of her dainty fist: *I'm jumping out of my skin.* You imagine your father, fiddling with his mustaches, fingering them a frazzle. You imagine Eloise (for surely they have called upon Eloise by now), tipsy, slurring, smiling, lying.

Why, she just left a few minutes ago.

Sprawling beneath these worries, throbbing, teeming, is, of course, your *experience.* You want nothing more than to retreat to your room, fling yourself on your bed, and delve into it. You feel the need to put your head back together, to reexamine the swarm of mysteries buzzing in your agitated wasp nest of a brain. But you are walking alone on the dark end of King Street in a narcotic daze, calculating the distance home, trying to figure out if it would be easier to get to Eloise's house. And now a drunk man pops up from a shrub, clownish and theatrical in the orb of a gas lantern, hat crooked, nose blighted, eyes twinkling with vaudevillian ferocity.

"Hello fine lady," he says.

You walk briskly. You hear him loping behind you. You think he might be gimp-legged, judging by the sloppy scrape of his shoes along the sidewalk, but you don't look back. When you sense him close and hot behind you, you break into a run, darting down Horlbeck Alley.

"Hello darling," a voice calls—young, rakish, male.

You hear a horse snort. You glance back, spot Everett Owling leering from Eloise's elegant little one-seater, clearly too drunk to manage a horse. Eloise perches beside him, her arms stretched wide.

You crawl up between them, fall into Eloise's arms, stifle an urge to sob.

"How was it?" she whispers.

"Still recovering," you say.

"Told you."

"My parents?"

"Taken care of." Eloise winks. "Besides, we'll all be gone next month. France, Italy, Turkey, then we'll sail across the Mediterranean to Egypt"

"The Sphinx is drowsy," says Everett, "her wings are furled."

Eloise rolls her eyes, jostles her cousin aside to take the reins.

You sink into the plush upholstery of Eloise's carriage and gaze up at the shimmer of stars. You see yourself walking on scorched sand. You see yourself ambling among ruins—aspiring arches, crumbling columns, pocked stone scoured by sun. You see yourself walking for hours, entering rooms without ceilings and furniture, savoring the blunt patterns of sun and shade, hoping that your head will finally clear, and you will know what to do next.

Page 5 (men on ladder). Harbison Agricultural College Collection, Accession no. 12525.118, Box 1.

Courtesy of South Caroliniana Library, University of South Carolina, Columbia, S.C.

A Long Way Up

bucket in hand
the first rung is for

sizing up
the vertical

glare cap chore
pause & pray

rung by rung
for the ladder to hold

let there be the ease
of a drainpipe

slipping over brick
& mortar

let there be let
there be no wind

one to lead one
the second man

grip grip or fall

LINDA LEE HARPER

Street scene. Beulah Glover Photograph Collection, Accession no. 12239.38, Folder 4.
Courtesy of South Caroliniana Library, University of South Carolina, Columbia, S.C.

Aunt Gloriana's Amen Sunday

She burns with passion for the natty dresser
who arrives in his classic car on Sunday
as her husband worships in church.
Gloriana's hunky lapse, steps up to the porch
tentative as a nervous preacher about to give
his first sermon, Gloriana's husband passing

collection plates to pew birds pious as
robed sopranos in the choir. Behind her
upstairs curtains, Gloriana's so tarted up
she could start grass fires as she passes.
Red-haired Aunt Gloriana who electrifies
nieces with her racy stories, her scandals

likely to erupt as spontaneously as the classic
car's gas tank that explodes, or is it Civil War
ordnance her fancy man haggled over at the tag
meet he hit before he shows up for bacon and bed
this hot July day? The blast torches the five
front-porch posts, the fringe of azaleas

consecrated holy bushes by their fiery glow
before the neighbor hoses them cold. Stained-
glass windows one mile away rattle, parishoners
praying for patience and peace, even as Gloriana
and her sweetie swoon in the bliss of stripping down
in air that's heated up, glass raining down

over their sheeted bower, breath a charred
trail from lips unlocking in that lava flow of light,
even the starling-studded telephone wires
melting, falling straight as a perfectly plum line
where the car's roof once curved and met
its double-pane windshield over the box of chocolates

the man forgot on the front seat which rests like an
abandoned divan in the middle of the cratered street,
the front porch screen blown inward, porch railing,
   spindles
splintered over the grass like painted kindling sparking
into tiny stars, a constellation of desire undone.

Since 1977, **GILBERT ALLEN** has lived on Paris Mountain and taught at Furman University, where he is the Bennette E. Geer Professor of Literature. His sixth collection of poems, *Catma,* is forthcoming. In April of 2014 Allen was inducted into the South Carolina Academy of Authors.

SAMUEL AMADON is the author of *The Hartford Book,* winner of the *Believer* Poetry Book Award, and *Like a Sea,* winner of the Iowa Poetry Prize. His poems have appeared recently in *The New Yorker, Poetry, American Poetry Review, Ploughshares, A Public Space,* and *Lana Turner.* He teaches in the M.F.A. program at the University of South Carolina, and edits *Oversound,* a poetry journal, with Liz Countryman.

LAUREL BLOSSOM'S second book-length narrative prose poem, *Longevity,* will be published in 2015 by Four Way Books, which also published *Degrees of Latitude* in 2007. Lyric collections include *Wednesday: New and Selected Poems, The Papers Said, What's Wrong,* and a chapbook, *Any Minute.* Her work has appeared in a number of anthologies, including *120 More: Extraordinary Poems for Every Day,* edited by Billy Collins; in *American Poetry Review, Poetry, Pequod, The Paris Review, Pleiades, xconnect,* and *Harper's,* among others; and online at friggmagazine.com, BigCityLit.com, Tupelo Quarterly 2, and elsewhere. Blossom has received fellowships

from the National Endowment for the Arts, the New York Foundation for the Arts, the Ohio Arts Council, and Harris Manchester College (Oxford University). Her poetry has been nominated for both the Pushcart Prize and the Elliston Prize.

DARIEN CAVANAUGH received his M.F.A. from the University of South Carolina. His work has been published or is forthcoming in *The Dos Passos Review, Memoir (and), The Blue Collar Review, The Coe Review, Struggle, Pank, The Blue Earth Review, The James Dickey Newsletter, Gertrude, I-70 Review, Rolling Thunder Quarterly, Kakalak, Burningword,* and *The San Pedro River Review.* He lives in Columbia, S.C., and works at the Whig.

PHEBE DAVIDSON is the author of twenty-some published collections of poems, most recently *Waking to Light* (2012), *Plasma Justice* (2011), and *Seven Mile* (2009). A new book of poems, *What Holds Him to this World,* has been chosen as a winner of the 2013 South Carolina Poetry Archive Book Prize and will be released later this spring by 96 Press. Davidson is a contributing editor at *Tar River Poetry* and a staff writer for *The Asheville Poetry Review.* Her book reviews, poems, and essays appear regularly in print and online. She has been nominated six times for a Pushcart Prize and holds a number of national poetry awards, among them the Kinloch Rivers,

Amelia, Soundpost Press, and Ledge Press manuscript prizes. A Distinguished Professor Emerita of the University of South Carolina Aiken, she thinks of herself as a recovering academic still up to her neck in poems.

PAM DURBAN is the author of a collection of short stories, *All Set About with Fever Trees,* and the novels *The Laughing Place, So Far Back,* and *The Tree of Forgetfulness.* Her short fiction has been published in many magazines and anthologies, including *The Best American Short Stories of the Century,* edited by John Updike. She is the recipient of a National Endowment for the Arts Creative Writing Fellowship and a Whiting Writer's Award as well as a James Michener Creative Writing Fellowship from the University of Iowa. Her novel, *So Far Back,* received the 2001 Lillian Smith Award for Fiction. Ms. Durban was born in Aiken, South Carolina, and attended the University of North Carolina at Greensboro and the University of Iowa Writer's Workshop. She teaches at the University of North Carolina in Chapel Hill, where she is the Doris Betts Distinguished Professor of Creative Writing.

JULIA ELLIOTT'S fiction has appeared in *Tin House, The Georgia Review, Conjunctions, Fence, Puerto del Sol, Mississippi Review,* and other magazines. She has won a Pushcart Prize and a Rona Jaffe Writer's Award. Her short story collection *The Wilds* was published in 2014, and her novel *The New and Improved Romie Futch* will follow in 2015. She is currently working on a novel about Hamadryas baboons, a species that she has studied as an amateur primatologist. She teaches English and women's and gender studies at the University of South Carolina in Columbia, where she lives with her daughter and husband. She and her spouse, John Dennis, are founding members of Grey Egg, an experimental music collective.

WORTHY EVANS is the winner of the 2009 South Carolina Poetry Prize for his book *Green Revolver* (University of South Carolina Press, 2010), Worthy Evans uses history, mythology, television, and everyday happenings in his life to inform his writing. After serving as a combat engineer between the wars (defending Fort Hood Texas from all assaults) Evans spent more than a decade with various newspapers in the state. When he isn't cutting up magazines and making collages, he serves as a communications specialist for a Medicare contractor in Columbia, S.C.

RICHARD GARCIA is the author of *Rancho Notorious* and *The Persistence of Objects,* and a chapbook of prose poems, *Chickenhead.* His poems have appeared in *The Georgia Review, Ploughshares, Pushcart Prize XXI, Best American Poetry* and in many anthologies. His manuscript, *The Other Odyssey,* was the 2012 winner of the American Poetry Journal book prize and is forthcoming. A collection of prose poems, *The Chair,* is also forthcoming. www.richardgarcia.info.

WILL GARLAND teaches English at the University of South Carolina, where he is a recent graduate of its M.F.A. program in creative writing. His work appears in *The Dead Mule School of Southern Literature, Real South Magazine, Black Fox Literary Magazine,* and other literary journals and anthologies. He was the recent winner of *One Columbia's* "One Book, One Poem" contest, judged by Ron Rash. He is also a staff writer for *Jasper Magazine,* and his work will be featured in Columbia's *Tiny Door Project* and the *Broadside Project.* William is currently working on a memoir that tells the story of a multi-generational struggle through family secrets and changing landscapes in Milledgeville, Georgia.

LINDA LEE HARPER'S *Kiss, Kiss* won CSU Poetry Center's Open Competition Winner and she has published seven chapbooks, including *Blue Flute.* She's received three Yaddo fellowships, four Pushcart nominations, and has published in over a hundred literary journals including *The Georgia Review, Nimrod, Beloit Poetry Journal, Rattle, Southern Poetry Review,* and others. She's written the libretto for Bambino, a baseball opera with Richard Maltz and divides time between Augusta, G.A. and Lake Murray, S.C.

TERRANCE HAYES is the author of *Lighthead,* winner of the 2010 National Book Award in poetry and finalist for the National Book Critics Circle Award. His honors include a Whiting Writers Award, a National Endowment for the Arts Fellowship, and a Guggenheim Fellowship. He is a professor of creative writing at the University of Pittsburgh.

THOMAS L. JOHNSON is a retired librarian emeritus from the University of South Carolina, where, as field archivist for the South Caroliniana Library, he was instrumental in the public rediscovery of the work of Columbia photographer Richard Samuel Roberts. *A True Likeness,* the book on Roberts's work co-edited by Johnson and Phillip C. Dunn (1986), won a coveted Lillian Smith Award from the Southern Regional Council. In 2002 he co-edited, with Nina J. Root, another book of photographs, *Camera Man's Jouney: Julian Dimock's South.* He has also been publishing prize-winning poetry since the 1970s. His collection *The Costume: New and Selected Poems* was published in 2010. Johnson currently lives in Spartanburg, where he has been active in the Hub City Writers Project, the Spartanburg Art Museum, and the West Main Artists Co-op (as a printmaker). He also serves on the board of the Birchwood Center for Arts and Folklife in Pickens County. He is a life member of the board of governors of the South Carolina Academy of Authors.

Currently a Ph.D. student in creative writing and literature at the University of Cincinnati, **JULIA KOETS'S** poetry has been published in *Indiana Review, The Los Angeles Review,* and *The Carolina Quarterly,* among others. Her first book of poetry, *Hold Like Owls,* won the 2011 South Carolina Poetry Book Prize (USC Press).

JOHN LANE is the author of a dozen books of poetry and prose. His latest, *Abandoned Quarry: New & Selected Poems,* was published in 2012. The book includes much of Lane's published poetry over the past 30 years, plus a selection of new poems. *Abandoned Quarry* won the SIBA (Southeastern Independent Booksellers Alliance) Poetry Book of the Year prize. His latest prose book is *Begin with Rock, End with Water* (2013). He is a co-founder of the Hub City Writers Project and teaches environmental studies at Wofford College. www.kudzutelegraph.com.

BRET LOTT is the *New York Times* bestselling author of thirteen books, most recently the novel *Dead Low Tide* (2012); other books include the story collection *The Difference Between Women and Men,* the nonfiction book *Before We Get Started: A Practical Memoir of the Writer's Life,* and the bestselling novels *Jewel,* an Oprah Book Club pick, and *A Song I Knew by Heart.* His work has appeared in, among other places, *The Yale Review, The New York Times, The Georgia Review* and in dozens of anthologies. Born in Los Angeles, he received his B.A. in English from Cal State Long Beach in 1981, and his M.F.A. in fiction from the University of Massachusetts, Amherst, in 1984, where he studied under James

Baldwin. From 1986 to 2004 he was writer-in-residence and professor of English at the College of Charleston, leaving to take the position of editor and director of the journal *The Southern Review* at Louisiana State University. Three years later, in the fall of 2007, he returned to the College of Charleston and the job he most loves: teaching. His has served as Fulbright Senior American Scholar and writer-in-residence to Bar-Ilan University in Tel Aviv, Israel; has spoken on Flannery O'Connor at the White House; and is a member of the National Council on the Arts. He and his wife, Melanie, live in Hanahan, South Carolina.

An associate professor of English at the University of South Carolina, **ED MADDEN** is the author of three books of poetry: *Signals* (2008), which won the 2007 SC Poetry Book Prize; *Prodigal: Variations* (2011); and *Nest* (2014). His work appears in *Best New Poets 2007, The Book of Irish American Poetry,* and *Hard Lines: Rough South Poetry.* He is the literary arts editor for *Jasper Magazine.*

JONATHAN MARICLE is a poet and communications consultant residing in Columbia, S.C. He earned an M.F.A. in poetry from the University of South Carolina and he is currently completing his Ph.D. in composition and rhetoric. After ten years in South Carolina there are many loves he has found anew: bourbon, Chairmen of the Board, rum punch, tea, and the smell of jasmine. And bourbon.

TERRI MCCORD has won awards from the South Carolina Poetry Initiative, the Poetry Society of South Carolina, the South Carolina Arts Commission, and various literary journals. Her poems can be found in *Seneca Review, Connecticut Review, Cimarron Review, Southeast Review,* and others as well as numerous anthologies and inclusion in the MUSC project.

She teaches as an adjunct at Anderson University and is an artist-in-residence. She has authored four poetry collections.

JANNA MCMAHAN is the national bestselling author of the novels *Anonymity, Calling Home* and *The Ocean Inside,* as well as the novella *Decorations.* Her short stories have won numerous awards such as the SC Fiction Project and the Piccolo Spoleto Fiction Open. Her fiction collection *Surface Tension,* was selected as a finalist for the Flannery O'Connor Award for Short Fiction. McMahan was recently chosen Literary Artist of the Year by the readers of *Jasper Magazine.*

RAY MCMANUS is the author of four books of poetry: *Red Dirt Jesus* (2011), *Left Behind* (2008), and *Driving through the country before you are born* (USC Press 2007). His fourth book, *Punch,* is forthcoming. Ray's poetry has appeared in many journals, most recently: *Blue Collar Review, Barely South, The Pinch, Hayden's Ferry,* and *moonShine Review.* Ray is the creative writing director for the Tri-District Arts Consortium in South Carolina, and he is an associate professor of English in the Division of Arts and Letters at University of South Carolina, Sumter, where he teaches creative writing, Irish literature, and Southern literature. www.raymcmanuspoetry.com.

SUSAN LAUGHTER MEYERS, of Givhans, S.C., is the author of two full poetry collections: *My Dear, Dear Stagger Grass* was recently published as the inaugural winner of the Cider Press Review Editors Prize; and *Keep and Give Away* (University of South Carolina Press) won the S.C. Poetry Book Prize and a SIBA Book Award. Her chapbook *Lessons in Leaving* received the Persephone Press Book Award. Her work has also appeared in *The Southern Review, Prairie Schooner, Crazyhorse,* and other journals and anthologies. A longtime writing instructor, she has an M.F.A. degree from Queens University of Charlotte.

MARK POWELL is the author of four novels, most recently *The Sheltering,* and has received fellowships from the National Endowment for the Arts and the Breadloaf Writers' Conference. A graduate of USC's M.F.A. program, he teaches at Stetson University in Florida.

MICHELE REESE is an associate professor of English at the University of South Carolina Sumter and the director for the South Carolina Center for Oral Narration. Her first book of poetry was *Following Phia.* Her poetry has appeared in *Congeries, The Paris Review, Grey Sparrow, Ithaca Lit,* and *American Athenaeum.*

JOHN MARK SIBLEY-JONES teaches English at the South Carolina Governor's School for the Arts and Humanities in Greenville, S.C. Prior to moving to Greenville, he taught English literature for fifteen years at the University of South Carolina, where he won several teaching awards, including the Michael A. Hill Outstanding Honors Faculty Award. Sibley-Jones has published more than fifty academic and professional articles, two short stories, and has been a finalist in several national fiction competitions. His first novel, *By the Red Glare,* a Civil War narrative, was published by USC Press in 2014.

GEORGE SINGLETON has published six collections of stories— *These People Are Us, The Half-Mammals of Dixie, Why Dogs Chase Cars, Drowning in Gruel, Stray Decorum,* and *Between Wrecks.* His two novels are *Novel* and *Workshirts for Madmen,* and his one book of writing advice is *Pep Talks, Warnings, and Screeds.* Singleton's short stories have appeared in *Atlantic Monthly, Harper's, Book, Playboy, Agni, Zoetrope, Georgia Review, Southern Review, Five Points, Oxford American, North American Review, New England Review, Fiction International, Ecotone, Virginia Quarterly Review, Carolina Quarterly,* and elsewhere. A 2009–10 Guggenheim fellowship recipient, Singleton received the 2011 Hillsdale Award from the Fellowship of Southern Writers, and was inducted in the South Carolina Academy of Authors in 2010. He holds the John C. Cobb Endowed Chair in the Humanities at Wofford College, in Spartanburg, SC.

CHARLENE SPEAREN holds an M.F.A. in creative writing and a Ph.D. in composition and rhetoric, each from the University of South Carolina. She is an assistant professor and Chair in the Humanities at Allen University, Columbia, S.C. She was awarded the 2012 South Carolina Independent Colleges and Universities Teacher of the Year Award for Allen University. She served as the Poet in Residence for the Columbia Museum of Art, and she has been awarded numerous residencies throughout the state of South Carolina. She was the program director for the University of South Carolina's Arts Institute (2005–2010) and the assistant director of the South Carolina's Poetry Initiative (2003–2011). Her full-length collection of poetry *A Book of Exquisite Disasters* (University of South Carolina Press, 2012) was favorably reviewed by Nikky Finney, 2011 National Book Award Winner. Her work has appeared in *Seeking: An Anthology of Poetry Responding to Jonathan Green's Seeking* (University of South Carolina Press, 2011), *-gape-seed* (2011), *Country Dog Review, The Southern Poetry Anthology: South Carolina* (2007), as well as other publications.

DANIEL NATHAN TERRY, a former landscaper and horticulturist, is the author of *Waxwings* (2012), *Capturing the Dead*

(2008), which won the Stevens Prize, and a chapbook, *Days of Dark Miracles* (2011). His poetry has appeared, or is forthcoming, in many journals and anthologies, including *Cimarron Review, New South, Poet Lore, Chautauqua,* and *Collective Brightness.* He serves on the advisory board of One Pause Poetry and teaches English at the University of North Carolina in Wilmington, where he lives with his husband, painter and printmaker Benjamin Billingsley.

JILLIAN WEISE is the author of *The Amputee's Guide to Sex,* the novel *The Colony,* and *The Book of Goodbyes,* which won the James Laughlin Award from the Academy of American Poets. She identifies as a cyborg. Her work has appeared in *The Atlantic, Narrative Inquiry in Bioethics, The New York Times,* and *Tin House.* She received fellowships from the Fine Arts Work Center, the Fulbright Program, and the University of North Carolina at Greensboro. She teaches at Clemson University.

MARJORY WENTWORTH'S poems have been nominated for the Pushcart Prize five times. Her books of poetry include *Noticing Eden, Despite Gravity,* and *The Endless Repetition of an Ordinary Miracle.* She is the co-writer with Juan Mendez of *Taking a Stand, The Evolution of Human Rights,* co-editor with Kwame Dawes of *Seeking, Poetry and Prose Inspired by the Art of Jonathan Green,* and the author of the prizewinning children's story *Shackles.* The University of South Carolina Press published her *New and Selected Poems* in 2014. Marjory teaches poetry in the Charleston County Schools Engaging Creative Minds Program, and she is on the faculty of the Art Institute of Charleston. She is the co-founder and president of the Lowcountry Initiative for the Literary Arts. Her work is included in the South Carolina Poetry Archives at Furman University, and she is the poet laureate of South Carolina.

WILLIAM WRIGHT, series editor and volume editor of *The Southern Poetry Anthology,* is author of six collections of poems: the full-length books *Tree Heresies* (forthcoming), *Night Field Anecdote* (2011), *Bledsoe* (2011), *Dark Orchard* (winner of the Texas Review Breakthrough Poetry Prize, 2005), and the chapbooks *Xylem & Heartwood* (2013), *Sleep Paralysis* (winner of the South Carolina Poetry Initiative Prize, 2011), and *The Ghost Narratives* (2008). Wright recently won the Porter Fleming Prize in Poetry. Recent work of Wright's appears in *Shenandoah, North American Review, Indiana Review, Colorado Review, Louisiana Literature, Beloit Poetry Journal, New Orleans Review,* and *Southern Poetry Review,* among other literary journals. In addition to writing and editing, Wright currently translates German poetry, particularly poems from the Austrian and German Expressionist period, and recent translations appear in *Nimrod International, Tampa Review,* and *Antioch Review.* Wright holds a Ph.D. in creative writing (poetry) and literature from the University of Southern Mississippi and is founding editor of *Town Creek Poetry* (www .towncreekpoetry.com).